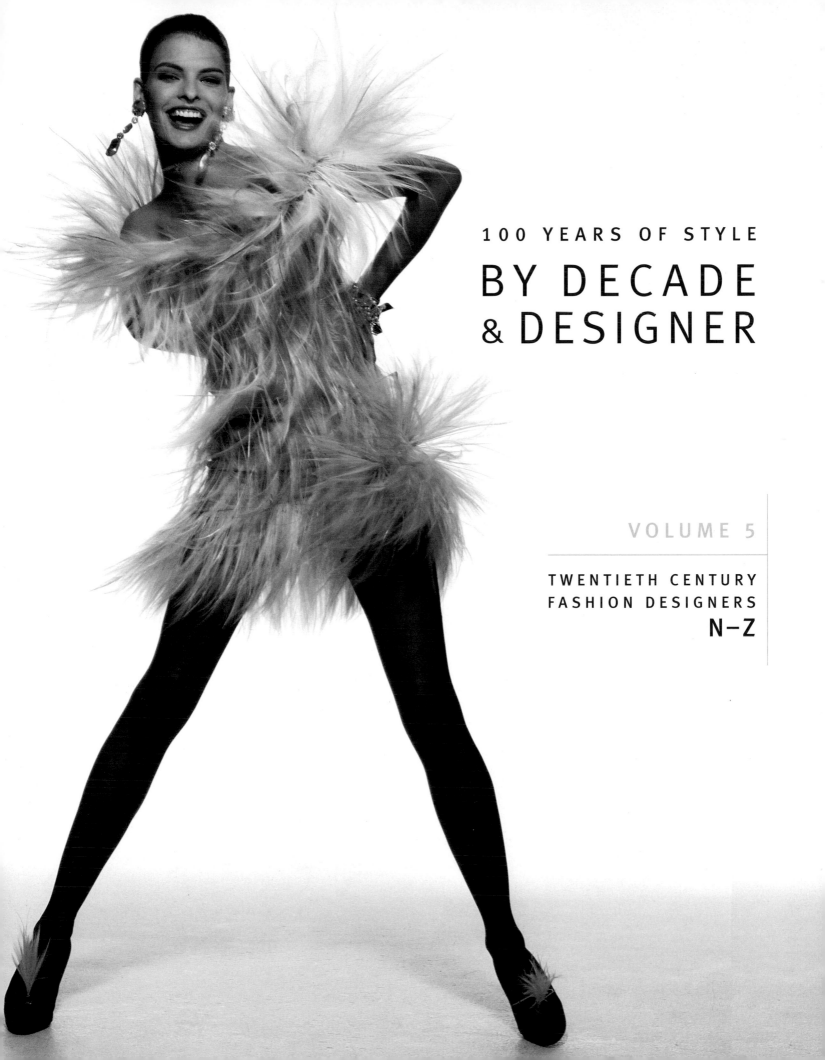

100 YEARS OF STYLE

# BY DECADE
# & DESIGNER

VOLUME 5

TWENTIETH CENTURY
FASHION DESIGNERS
**N–Z**

This edition copyright 2001 by Chelsea House Publishers, a subsidiary of Haights Cross Communications. Printed and bound in Dubai.

First printing

1 3 5 7 9 8 6 4 2

The Chelsea House World Wide Web address is
http://www.chelseahouse.com

Library of Congress Cataloging-in-Publication Data applied for


ISBN 0 7910 6196 5 Fashion Designers N–Z (this edition)

0 7910 6192 2 Fashions 1900–1949
0 7910 6193 0 Fashions 1950–1999
0 7910 6194 9 Fashion Designers A–F
0 7910 6195 7 Fashion Designers G–M
0 7910 6191 4 (set)



Produced by Carlton Books
20 Mortimer Street
London W1N 7RD

Text and Design copyright © Carlton Books Limited 1999/2000

Photographs copyright © 1999 Condé Nast Publications Limited

Previous page: Yellow and pale ostrich-feathered slip of flesh-coloured muslin, accessorized by barley sugar glass drop earrings, 1987.

Opposite: A typically outrageous statement – silk swags and fake fur – from Vivienne Westwood in 1991, the year she was voted British Designer of the Year.

Overleaf: Marisa Berenson wears Emilio Pucci's stretch bikini and matching velvet robe, printed with opulent patterns and grandly clashing colours, 1968.

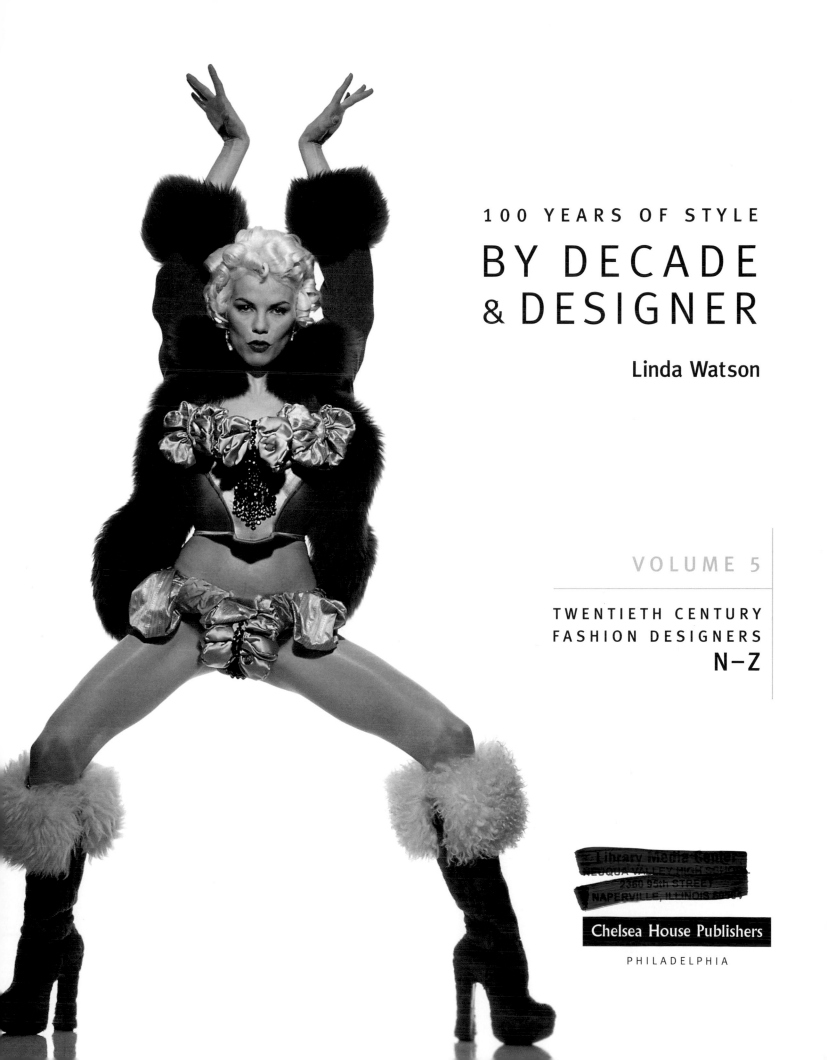

100 YEARS OF STYLE
# BY DECADE
# & DESIGNER

Linda Watson

VOLUME 5

TWENTIETH CENTURY
FASHION DESIGNERS
N–Z

Chelsea House Publishers

PHILADELPHIA

# contents

# NORELL, Norman

BORN: NOBLESVILLE, INDIANA, USA, 1900
DIED: NEW YORK, NEW YORK, USA, 1972

Called the 'dramatist of New York designers' in his heyday, Norman Norell was the legendary minimalist of American design. Isaac Mizrahi, an ardent admirer, described his design in *Vogue* magazine as 'so egoless, simply the most glamorous clothes said in the fewest words'.

Norell was a sickly child. His mother was the fashion plate in his native Noblesville, which had a population of 5,000. The Norell family moved to Indianapolis when he was 5 years old. On leaving high school he enlisted with the military, and at 19 he enrolled at Parson's School of Design in New York. He left on a whim to open a batik shop, before returning to study fashion at New York's Pratt Institute, where he was awarded first prize in a blouse competition, winning $100 in the process.

Norell left the Pratt Institute believing that costume design was his destiny, and through a connection in the film industry worked with Valentino, Gloria Swanson and Greenwich Village Follies. This last position led to jobs with Brooks Costume Company, Charles Armour and in 1928, Hattie Carnegie, where he remained for 13 years, travelling with her to Europe, where he was exposed to the best designs of the day.

In 1941 he founded Triana-Norell with clothing manufacturer Anthony Triana. From the very first collection under the new label, Norell established himself as a major new talent. His logical mind led to the creation of fur trousers, cut to a shorter, more manageable length, and jersey shifts. He also pioneered the wearing of black and white when American women were wearing a uniform of florals.

Over the years Norell continued to set numerous trends that have become part of our fashion vocabulary today. He was the first to show long evening skirts topped with sweaters; he revived the chemise and perfected jumpers and pantsuits. In the tradition of American design, Norell had conviction, a sublime understanding of understatement and a talent for originality without alienation. He detested superfluous detail unless, as he commented at the time, 'it has a darn good reason'.

LEFT **The ultimate American classicist: Norman Norell's 'deep new, deep slit' dress of 1967, with very low front. The long skirt reveals a length of leg.**

# NUTTER, Tommy

BORN: LONDON, ENGLAND, 1943
DIED: LONDON, ENGLAND, 1992

Tommy Nutter spearheaded the radical shake-up of London's sleepy Savile Row in the 1960s, taking traditional clothes and turning them into fashion statements; he dressed every mover and shaker on the circuit.

Nutter's introduction into the fashion world was unconventional to say the least. He studied plumbing at Willesden Technical College and originally worked in the building trade before taking a tailoring apprenticeship at Donaldson, Williams & Ward in Burlington Arcade, London. In 1968 Tommy Nutter positioned himself in Savile Row, dressing the hip aristocracy – John Lennon and Yoko Ono, Mick and Bianca Jagger – as well as the traditionalists – Hardy Amies and the Earl of Snowdon.

Nutter was an expert self-publicist, dispensing off-the-cuff comments on the correct buttoning, the minutiae of English fabric and how he had single-handedly shaken up Savile Row. He ventured into ready to wear in 1978 under the Austin Reed label. Examples of his suiting are housed in Bath Museum of Costume in England and Los Angeles Museum of Art in the USA.

# OLDFIELD, Bruce

BORN: LONDON, ENGLAND, 1950

The most famous Barnado's boy in the world, Bruce Oldfield was brought up by a Miss Masters in Durham, England, until the age of 13. At 7 years old, his case history read, 'Violet Masters firmly believes this boy will become a fashion designer.'

Oldfield fulfilled his foster mother's prediction. He fought his way into Central Saint Martins College of Art and Design in London, and established his own company. His first *Vogue* cover appeared in the 1970s, featuring a couple intertwined with a pair of Manolo Blahnik shoes. Oldfield's style is sexy and feminine. He has dressed many celebrities, including Charlotte Rampling, Catherine Zeta Jones and Jemima Goldsmith at her wedding to Imran Khan in 1995, but his most famous client was Diana, Princess of Wales, for whom he made many frocks including a turquoise and silver ruffled evening dress, which she wore on her Australian tour of 1983.

Awarded an OBE in 1990, Oldfield has survived the vagaries of taste through a combination of skill, charm and steely determination. 'I have been in and out of fashion more times than I remember,' he said after 20 years in business. 'Fashion and clients are fickle.'

ABOVE **Oldfield's ivory-silk dupion sleeveless top, with an ivory and burnt sienna full skirt, 1996.**

# OLDHAM, Todd

BORN: CORPUS CHRISTI, TEXAS, USA, 1961

Todd Oldham is the innovative man behind America's most outlandish label – a designer who started his career in fashion doing alterations in a Dallas department store, before moving to New York in 1988 where he started his Times 7 line. He has collaborated with artists Kenny Scharf and Ruben Toledo, and is best known for his use of colour and erratic prints.

Oldham takes simple shapes and adds unconventional touches. He is expert at surface decoration: sequins, trompe l'oeil and unusual buttons, which metamorphose into animated dresses. He is vehemently anti-fur – his conviction extends to appearing naked in advertisements to underline his case. In 1991, at the age of 30, Oldham received the CFDA Perry Ellis Award for New Fashion Talent.

# ORRY-KELLY

BORN: SYDNEY, AUSTRALIA, 1898
DIED: HOLLYWOOD, USA, 1964

Orry-Kelly is responsible for the wonderful opening scene of *The Gold Diggers of 1933*. when a host of Hollywood lovelies run riot across the screen singing, 'We're in the Money', and wearing costumes constructed from coins. His Oscar-winning work includes his costume for *Les Girls* (1957) and the Marilyn Monroe classic, *Some Like It Hot* (1959).

Born Walter Orry Kelly (the film studio dropped the Walter and added a hyphen), he migrated from Australia to America in 1923 with the intention of becoming an actor. He began a career in costume design via illustrating titles for silent movies and a friendship with Cary Grant, eventually becoming a designer at Warner Brothers. He stayed there from 1923–43, during which time he designed for Bette Davis in *Jezebel* (1938) and *The Little Foxes* (1941). He also designed the cream satin wedding dress she wore in *The Old Maid* (1939) and costumed the Humphrey Bogart classic *Casablanca* (1942). In 1943 Orry-Kelly moved to Twentieth-century Fox, then Universal Studios, and finally MGM.

RIGHT **'Newest arrival in the strong tradition of architect-turned-dress designer': Turkish-born Rifat Ozbek's frilled shirt, capri pants and sock hat, 1986.**

# OZBEK, Rifat

BORN: ISTANBUL, TURKEY, 1953

Rifat Ozbek travelled from Istanbul to Liverpool to study architecture and then switched to fashion at Central Saint Martins College of Art and Design in London. His first job was at Monsoon and he later established his own company. Ozbek's clever use of Moroccan colour and embroidery – often accessorized with a fez – prompted *Vogue*'s Grace Coddington to comment in 1986: 'At the moment dance is in the air and so is Rifat. He's done a collection where the ballet theme goes right through – but it's not exaggerated, it's immensely wearable *and* fun.' *Women's Wear Daily* was equally effusive, calling his collection 'a healthy dose of the unexpected'. In 1987 Ozbek launched the Future Ozbek diffusion line, and in 1990 he presented a pure white collection and made a video in conjunction with film director John Maybury. Quiet, low-key and rarely seen on the fashion circuit, Ozbek showed his sense of humour when he parodied ex-*Vogue* editor Diana Vreeland in *Tatler*, with a necklace made from spanners from photographer David Bailey's tool box. The fashion directive was: 'Think Sink!'

# PAQUIN

FOUNDED BY JEANNE BECKERS AND ISIDORE JACOBS IN 1891

When it was founded, the house of Paquin was situated in modest quarters at 3 rue de la Paix in Paris, but soon occupied the whole building. Jeanne Beckers learnt her craft working for Maggy Rouff, and Isidore Jacobs acquired his business skills on the Bourse (the couple became known as Monsieur and Madame Paquin). By 1915 the export trade had been sufficiently explored to enable Paquin to open in London, Madrid, Buenos Aires and New York. Beckers was the company's best advertisement – tall and beautiful, *Vogue* described her as 'a mother-of-pearl woman. She has the will of a man and is a genius in business organisation.' Her personal fortune was estimated at four million francs. She appeared regularly at Longchamp and Chantilly, averting all eyes from the horses and keeping the copyists in jobs. Unsure of which direction the house should take, she turned to Paul Iribe and Léon Bakst, but their contribution was not a success. Rated by *Vogue* as 'definitely in the first rank of the Grandes Maisons', Paquin was internationally known for its dexterity in mixing evening fabrics with fur – such as wraps in matt-white crepe, edged with sable.

ABOVE **Paquin's crepe georgette dress with a bloused bodice, snug girdle and wrinkled sleeves, 1925: 'very much of the present moment, full of interesting points'.**

# PATOU, Jean

**BORN: NORMANDY, FRANCE, 1880**
**DIED: PARIS, FRANCE, 1936**

Jean Patou established his business during the First World War and opened his salon on the rue Saint Florentin just after Armistice Day. His shows were one of the social high points of Paris in the early 1930s, where the audience was a blend of 'buyers and silk manufacturers, diplomats, artists and smart ladies, presenting a company as amusing as any first night of a new play'. In 1932 Patou dropped the waistline and revived the classic Moyen-Âge silhouette. The result was assessed as 'dreams of beauty', with *Vogue* reiterating: 'Patou states that it was not as a couturier, but as a man that he designs his costumes.'

By 1950 the house had branches in Monte Carlo, Deauville and Venice, and was directed by Patou's sister and her husband, Madame and Monsieur Barbas. 'The house still caters to a distinguished Old World clientele, and is still outstanding for its fine workmanship and hand details,' said *Vogue* in 1950.

# PEARCE FIONDA

**FOUNDED BY REN PEARCE AND ANDREW FIONDA IN 1994**

Two fashion graduates from Nottingham Trent University, who joined forces after completing their respective MAs, Ren Pearce and Andrew Fionda describe their style as 'very modern eveningwear, mixed with tailoring. We always balance it within the collection.' Pearce had previously worked with John Galliano and Roland Klein, Fionda with high street giants Marks and Spencer and Alexon. Together they make clothes which have caught the imagination of Nicole Kidman and Iman. Winners of major awards such as New Generation and Glamour from the British Fashion Council, and the World Young Designer's Award in Turkey, they told *Vogue* in 1998: 'We're not interested in tricksy street fashion. We want to offer women sophisticated, grown-up clothes.'

# PERTEGAZ, Manuel

**BORN: ARAGON, SPAIN, 1918**

A Spanish designer of elegant, refined eveningwear, Manuel Pertegaz is known for his simplistic approach and lack of ostentation. Pertegaz became a tailor's apprentice and opened his own salon in Barcelona in 1942. He became world famous, as well as a household name in his native Spain, for his dexterity in both the couture and ready-to-wear markets. He was a couturier in the Cristobal Balenciaga tradition – if flounces were used, they had a subtlety which combined Spanish flair with Parisian control. His tailoring was understated and easy – curved to give the illusion of fit. Pertegaz was one of the first Spanish designers to be featured in *Vogue* in the early 1950s – the 'newest of the European fashion groups to make their influence felt on an international scale' – and often talked about in the same sentence as Emilio Pucci.

# PERUGIA, André

**BORN: NICE, FRANCE, 1893**
**DIED: CANNES, FRANCE, 1977**

An original master craftsman, André Perugia is the shoemaker most admired by his modern-day equivalent, Manolo Blahnik. The son of a shoemaker, Perugia excelled in the absolute precise proportions of couture footwear. The inward curve of the heel perfectly echoed the position of the straps; corkscrew heels created a balance between fantasy and comfort. Of Italian and French parentage, Perugia opened his own shop in Nice when he was 16 years old. He was commissioned to provide shoes for Paul Poiret and Elsa Schiaparelli, and later for the collections of Hubert de Givenchy and Jacques Fath. He also shod Hollywood stars and aristocrats. His surrealist tendencies – outlandish designs that were still wearable – ran parallel to his more understated shoes. Thanks to his solid grounding as a craftsman, Perugia was able to produce fantastical creations which did not cause undue discomfort.

# PIGUET, Robert

**BORN: YVERDON, SWITZERLAND, 1901**
**DIED: LAUSANNE, SWITZERLAND, 1953**

Heralded by *Vogue* as 'master of the little wool dress', Robert Piguet was a pupil of Paul Poiret's and an employee of John Redfern's before he branched out on his own prior to the Second World War. Piguet – who had Poiret's colour sense, but a less ornate approach – designed for chic Parisians who wore dresses with matching jackets, crisp coats and romantic evening gowns.

OPPOSITE **Walking the dog in Deauville, 1927, in Patou's two-piece bathing suit 'cut down very much at the back for sunbathing'.**

# PINET, François

BORN: CHÂTEAU-LE-VAILLÈRE, FRANCE, 1817
DIED: FRANCE, 1897

Trained in the complex art of shoemaking by his father, François Pinet arrived in Paris and quickly became known as shoemaker to the chic. In 1861 he won the Nantes Prize and in 1863 he opened an establishment on the rue Paradis Poissonnière. Pinet developed his own style of heel – an elegant, slimline version of the norm that was christened, naturally enough, the Pinet heel.

# PLUNKETT, Walter

BORN: OAKLAND, CALIFORNIA, USA, 1902
DIED: 1982

Most famous for his costumes for Vivien Leigh as Scarlett O'Hara in the cinematic classic *Gone with the Wind* (1939), Walter Plunkett was a specialist in historical costume. He reduced Leigh's waist from 23 inches to 18 inches, tactfully saying: 'We know how to give the illusion of a small waist in the pictures – that's all part of costuming.'

Plunkett learnt his craft on the vaudeville circuit; he went to Hollywood in 1925 and danced in Erich von Stroheim's *The Merry Widow*. He was eventually appointed within the costume design department of FBO (later RKO), designing costumes for the early Fred Astaire and Ginger Rogers musicals, including *The Gay Divorcee* (1934). Plunkett left RKO in 1934 to pursue a freelance career, costuming Katharine Hepburn in *Mary of Scotland* (1936). He later joined MGM, where his two most famous productions were *Singin' In The Rain* (1952) and *Seven Brides for Seven Brothers* (1954). In 1951 he won an Oscar for his work on *An American in Paris* (1951).

# POIRET, Paul

BORN: PARIS, FRANCE, 1879
DIED: PARIS, FRANCE, 1947

Paul Poiret was the twentieth century's most dazzling *enfant terrible*. An incurable Orientalist, he brought opulence, a new silhouette and a sense of elegance which has never been equalled. His vision shaped

LEFT **Poiret's suit 'for a tailleur with an air'. Overlapping pointed coat, cire collar and starched ruff running down the front, 1922.**

LEFT 'Gay patterns find great favour' in Poiret's celebration of geometry – coral-coloured gaberdine suit with Russian jumper and white belt, 1924.

BELOW Poiret's advertisement in *Vogue*, 1924, complete with constructivist typography; he was one of the fashion world's first and most brilliant self-publicists.

Poiret was instrumental in stabilizing the Parisian fashion industry. It was his idea to form the Syndicat de Défense de la Grande Couture Française, of which he became president. It was also he who made the unprecedented move to exhibit Parisian collections – both his and those of his contemporaries – in the USA. Poiret was the first designer to understand the value of public relations, personally presenting collections in London. He was also a keen driver and collaborated with Renault cars in advertisements.

Poiret travelled to Russia and the Far East in search of original fabrics. He adored Chinese art, spoke several languages and delivered lectures in English. He could play the piano and the violin; he also painted portraits and wrote poetry. When the First World War broke out, Poiret, then in his late thirties, was among the first reservists called to serve in the French infantry. His house

the way we dress now. By his own admission he 'freed the bust but shackled the legs'. A former pupil of Charles Worth and Jacques Doucet, Poiret first attracted the attention of the press in 1903 when he staged a presentation in a shop in rue Auber, Paris, where, to an audience constricted by sinuous corsets and boned necklines, he showed dresses decorated with autumn leaves and Oriental embroideries.

In 1905 Poiret married Denise Boulet – a natural beauty from Normandy and an advocate of aesthetic dress. Breaking the mould of conventional couture, he positioned his salon in the quartier de l'Opéra on l'avenue d'Antin and rue du Faubourg-Saint-Honoré. The house was elegant inside and out, with a lawn patterned in the manner of André Le Nôtre (who designed the gardens at Versailles), a gravelled drive and a uniformed Swiss guard. The salons were spread with lush red carpets and tricolour silks; the models – gorgeous figurines in Poiret's vision of Orientalism – filed silently through. 'All this combines to create a fearsome air of luxury in which the most prudent female minds lose the sense of economy and yield themselves to the sheer intoxication of elegance,' said *Vogue*, obviously seduced by his 1915 collection.

*Late September*

# PAVL POIRET

WILL

## PERSONALLY PRESENT

HIS

## WINTER CREATIONS

ON

THVRSDAY OCTOBER 2ND

AT 3. P.M.

AT

## YVONNE CHASTEL LIMITED

## 7 ALBEMARLE ST. W. I.

TELEPHONE GERRARD 7560

ADMISSION BY TICKET ONLY

OBTAINABLE IN ADVANCE

closed for the duration of the war and when it re-opened, the economic situation was radically different. This had a catastrophic effect on the designer, who lived for luxury. Poiret persevered – personally presenting his collection in London during the mid-1920s. However, he had to face the fact that his talent for beauty no longer applied to the new, more streamlined, look. Struggling to survive in a world which had moved on to plainer clothes and abbreviated lines, Poiret died penniless in 1947.

# PORTER, Thea

**BORN: JERUSALEM, ISRAEL, 1927**

For Thea Porter read: bohemian, advocate of flower power and free-thinker. She made ethnic clothes for hippie sensibilities, with flowing lines, seductive colours and lavish surface textures. Part-hippie, part-dreamer, her ethereal clothes often combined cultural influences – a Nehru collar with a flounced sleeve – and reflected the bohemian tendencies of the time.

Porter spent her childhood in Damascus. She studied French and then art at London University. In 1967 she opened her own boutique, selling exotic textiles and, later, her own clothes. Porter concentrated on simple lines and exotic fabrics – panne velvet, brocade, crepe de Chine and chiffon. Her forte was the full-length evening dress or kaftan. In 1971 she collaborated with Hungarian fabric designer, Michael Szell to produce her 'romantic and ravishing evening dresses'. Later, she became both a dress and interior designer, working on a freelance basis.

RIGHT **Thea Porter's black fur coat, appliquéd with a mosaic of Beirut carpet embroidery, worn with ethnic bag and chunky embroidered boots, 1970.**

# PRADA

**FOUNDED BY MARIO PRADA IN 1913**

It would be simplistic to say that Prada built its empire on a nylon bag, but during the 1990s the infamous black bag with its simple silver insignia became the fashion editor's favourite and a phenomenal money-spinner. Since then, Prada has concentrated more on clothes, and the look is in line with the company's design directive: discreet labels and refined tailoring. Young enough for the twentysomethings and sufficiently non-threatening to the over-thirties, Prada has a strong sense of self and is now headed by Miuccia Prada, the granddaughter of the founder, who has a PhD in political science and is a patron of the arts; she also has an astute marketing mind. Although it was founded as a leather goods company in 1913, Miuccia, who took over in the 1970s has helped make the Prada name known internationally: there are flagship stores in New York and London, and in 1992 the diffusion line, Miu Miu, was added to the Prada portfolio.

OPPOSITE **Technological fabrics given the Prada treatment in 1998: satin and latex top, waxed cotton pedal pushers and very high-heeled linen mules.**

# PRICE, Antony

BORN: KEIGHLEY, ENGLAND, 1945

One of the first designers to bridge the gap between fashion and pop music, Antony Price was instrumental in directing and designing the look of seminal rock band Roxy Music in the 1970s. Brilliant at building characters, constructing stage sets and re-drawing uniforms, Price dressed Bryan Ferry as a dashing GI and a debonair gigolo. One of his tongue-in-cheek outfits was dubbed 'The Spanish Traffic Warden', and he also turned Jerry Hall into a mermaid wrapped around the rocks. 'I love putting together videos for Roxy,' he told *Vogue* in 1980. 'I can play Cecil B De Mille on a small scale. It's a bit of old Hollywood – all the glamour, the rocks, the posing.'

Price trained at Bradford School of Art, before moving on to study fashion at the Royal College of Art in London. He worked as a designer with Stirling Cooper, then Plaza, and opened his own shop in London's King's Road in 1980. The stark new outlet was simply designed and lit with soft shades of violet.

Price's customers have always been rock stars, the wives of rock stars, and wannabees. His structured dresses are designed to make an impact, and he doesn't know the meaning of the phrase 'dressing down'. Dubbed 'The Leader of the Glam' by *Vogue* in 1990, and once rumoured to be in line for a position at Versace, Price told *The Sunday Times* in 1998: 'God comes in the shape of an Italian factory and if he doesn't you're f****d.'

RIGHT **Famed for his 'result wear', Antony Price's gold dress of 1980 has curvy lines, vampish tendencies, and a touch of Hollywood.**

# PUCCI, Marchese Emilio

BORN: NAPLES, ITALY, 1914
DIED: FLORENCE, ITALY, 1992

Worn by Marilyn Monroe and a variety of other twentieth-century sex bombs, Pucci has metamorphosed from Italian print to cult pattern in the latter part of the century and is collected and coveted by supermodels and fashion cognoscenti. At the core of the Pucci look is its distinctive colour and bold, swirling patterns. *Vogue* christened the designer 'Pucci, the print maestro'. Educated in Milan and Florence in Italy and Georgia and Oregon in the USA, Emilio Pucci served as a pilot in the Italian air force during the Second World War and had a long-term interest in politics, serving two terms in the Italian Chamber of Deputies in the 1950s. He entered the world of fashion after being photographed on the ski slopes by Toni Frissell of *Harper's Bazaar*, wearing ski pants of his own design. On the strength of the interest these attracted, the magazine asked him to create some winter clothes for women, which were subsequently sold in stores in New York.

Pucci prints came to epitomize Italian colour and the post-war movement; they were perfect for the psychedelic 1950s. Pucci's greatest work was the shirt, which whirled on the body and was often bordered with graphic patterning. Later, came a range of accessories including scarves and silk handbags. Pucci's palazzo pyjamas were worn with jewelled sandals and described in 1964 as, 'Equally at home in the palazzo and at parties that end at dawn; they speak of an atmosphere that's rareified – sun-tossed, and moonlit.'

During the 1990s, newly directed by Pucci's daughter Laudomia, the label enjoyed a renaissance with the famously vivid patterns appearing on Lycra leggings rather than silk shirts.

OPPOSITE **Marisa Berenson wears Emilio Pucci's stretch bikini and matching velvet robe, printed with opulent patterns and grandly clashing colours, 1968.**

# QUANT, Mary

**BORN: LONDON, ENGLAND, 1934**

Widely credited with inventing the miniskirt, Mary Quant doesn't lay claim to designing what was already in the air. Much more importantly, she took the mini (then in its infancy) and marketed it – making it the most potent symbol of the 1960s.

Together with her husband, Alexander, who she met at London's Goldsmith's Art College, Quant opened her shop, Bazaar, in London in 1955; underneath it was her husband's restaurant. Quant had a cataclysmic effect on London, with her simple daisy motif, short skirts, mix of music and model, Twiggy. By 1963 she was famous enough to have made an impression on American *Vogue*, who called her an English adventurer in London: 'She looks like one of those wispy child heroines – leggy, skinny, with soup-bowl bangs, very pale painted mouth, heavy black liner on upper and lower lashes,' the magazine wrote. Immediately after her first trip to the USA, Quant launched her Ginger Group – a less expensive line of mix-and-match coordinates, including knickerbockers and waistcoats, assessed by *Vogue* in 1963 as, 'a snowball of a wardrobe … that will mix and match up endlessly'. In 1966 Quant had built up a multi-million pound business, written her autobiography *Quant by Quant*, and been awarded an OBE. In 1970 she gave birth to her son, Orlando, and had moved on from designing for adolescent proportions to designing interiors. Her internationally known name and logo, associated with youth and freshness, enabled her to change direction and encompass kitchenware, stationery and fabulous make-up.

By 1977 Quant had a holiday house in Nice, and had relocated to Surrey with her husband and son, and a Jaguar 'with a large dent'. Elected into the British Fashion Hall of Fame, the Quant name has transcended into fashion folklore.

# RABANNE, Paco

BORN: SAN SEBASTIÁN, SPAIN, 1934

Called 'Wacko Paco', and an assortment of other names which basically mean 'lost the plot', Paco Rabanne was a designer of seriously radical dresses during the 1960s. It is only recently that he has metamorphosed into a blatant attention-seeker.

In 1939 Rabanne left Spain, eventually ending up in Brittany, France. He trained as an architect, switched to fashion and started making jewellery. Rabanne made a real impact on 1960s fashion, with his signature use of plastic discs inter-linked with wire, and love of sharp shapes. In 1966 he hit the headlines with his futuristic use of multicoloured plastic discs (with matching earrings), chain mail, and aluminium diamonds on eveningwear. He then progressed to moulded dresses and furniture. In between man landing on the moon and the millennium, however, he lost his way. Or rather he decided to re-write history and reinvent himself at the same time. Today, Rabanne talks little of fashion and clothes and more of astral travels, guardian angels and good vibrations. In 1999 he used his heavenly powers to predict that President Chirac would be assassinated, and that the last eclipse of the millennium would herald the destruction of Paris. Chirac, as we go to press, is still alive and kicking. Ditto: Paris.

He produced his final collection in July 1999, which featured a satellite dress, mirrors and other flying objects. He has also published two books, *Journey – From One Life to Another* (1997) and *Dawn of the Golden Age*; *A Spiritual Design for Living* (1999), both filled with celestial musings on all matters mystical.

# RAYNE, Sir Edward

BORN: LONDON, ENGLAND, 1922
DIED: EAST SUSSEX, ENGLAND, 1992

Edward Rayne served a lengthy apprenticeship in the factory of his family's firm, H&M Rayne, learning all about the complexities of making shoes. In 1951, at the age of 29, Rayne became managing director of the business which had been founded by his grandparents in 1889. Under Rayne's direction the company – with three royal

warrants – grew into an international concern, with licensing deals with American department stores Bonwit Teller and Bergdorf Goodman.

In 1960 Rayne was appointed chairman of the Incorporated Society of London Fashion Designers; later, when it became the British Fashion Council, he became its president for five years. Awarded a CVO in 1977 and knighted in 1988, Sir Edward was instrumental in putting British fashion back on course, and for generating international interest. Jean Muir called him, 'the best British shoemaker of his age'.

# REBOUX, Caroline

BORN: *c* 1830
DIED: PARIS, FRANCE, 1927

A major player in the history of millinery, Caroline Reboux was credited simply with the name 'Reboux', which became synonymous with chic hats throughout the early part of this century. With an instinctive French flair for shape and form, Reboux collaborated with Madeleine Vionnet and had many high-profile clients.

# REDFERN

### FOUNDED BY JOHN REDFERN IN 1881

English tailor, John Redfern, established himself in Paris in 1881 with a salon on the rue de Rivoli. He was appointed dressmaker to Queen Victoria in 1888 and created the first women's uniform for the Red Cross in 1916. Redfern caused a furore by making eye-catching costumes for Jane Hading in the role of Madame de Pompadour: 'He is both conservative and very individual, and has always had a clientele who hate banality,' *Vogue* wrote in 1923.

Redfern's full-page advertisement of 1920 cited branches in London, Paris, Nice and Monte Carlo. 'Costumes for the races, Gowns for Henley, Gowns and cloaks for their Majesties Courts, millinery for all occasions, furs and lingerie,' read the copy. Redfern's customers included Sarah Bernhardt and Madame Pierat, with whom he collaborated at the Théâtre Français. His royal front row included the Queen of Romania (who committed the fashion faux pas of wearing a black Lanvin coat for the presentation of his autumn 1920 collection). What they saw was typically Redfern: long coats which nodded to the style of the last century, a suit called Grand Siècle and fur coats of mole, kolinsky and mink. *Vogue*'s headline read 'Redfern Opens Brilliantly'. The slightly historic collection harked back to the fifteenth and eighteenth centuries. Among Redfern's specialities were a short, fur-trimmed overcape, a camel-hair suit, brocade dresses and draped satin.

# RHODES, Zandra

### BORN: CHATHAM, ENGLAND, 1940

A self-confessed workaholic who has followed her own vision since the 1960s, Zandra Rhodes lives, eats, sleeps and breathes textiles. 'I've had six or seven original ideas in my life and that's all,' she admitted to *Vogue* in 1978. 'With me, it's fifteen per cent talent, and the rest is sloggin' your guts out.'

Rhodes, who believes 'showmanship *is* the business', has one of the strongest identities in the industry. She has brightly coloured hair, dramatic make-up and imaginative dresses which are indisputably her own design. Her signatures include zigzags, lipsticks, Art Deco motifs, stars and teardrops. Adored in America, Rhodes's clothes have been bought and worn by a variety of women, from Tina Chow to Vanessa Redgrave. Her royal contributions have included Princess Anne's engagement dress, and eveningwear for Diana, Princess of Wales. In December 1998 she made a pink-haired fairy for the royal Christmas tree.

Rhodes – eternally grateful that her parents put a 'Z' instead of an 'S' in her name – is the daughter of a lorry driver and an art teacher. She spent her childhood copying illustrations from Cicely Mary Barker's *Flower Fairy* books. Rhodes studied textile printing and lithography at Medway College and then at the Royal College of Art in London, which she left in 1964. By 1969 her designs were appearing in *Vogue*. In 1970 she dyed her hair green.

First and foremost Rhodes is a textile designer, creating handscreened fabrics such as chiffon, tulle and silk; she has always designed her clothes around the pattern, never the other way around. Her portfolio of achievements is impressive: she has exhibited in Australia, Tokyo, Paris and Manchester; her clothes are housed in museums from Brighton to Chicago. She has lectured from Colorado to Kansas. Her most recent project is the building of a Fashion and Textile Museum in Bermondsey. In 1995 she received a Hall of Fame Award from the British Fashion Council; in 1996 she was given a Lifetime Achievement Award in California, and in 1997 a CBE – all richly-deserved accolades for the woman the *Los Angeles Times* once called, 'London's lovely fashion lunatic'.

# RICCI, Nina

### BORN: TURIN, ITALY, 1883
### DIED: PARIS, FRANCE, 1970

A respected house, which opened in 1932, the Nina Ricci label has become synonymous with impeccable taste and French refinement. Born in Turin, Ricci relocated to France as an adolescent and from the age of 13 undertook a traditional apprenticeship with a couturier, learning the intricacies of making couture garments. Supported by her husband, a jeweller, she opened her house at a time when Elsa Schiaparelli and Coco Chanel were grabbing the headlines and surrealism was the word on everyone's lips. Admired for her technical skills and high standards, Ricci specialized in the complete look, rather than individual experiments or ground-breaking statements, and the elegant, graceful clothes that her house produced became popular with sophisticated women. The house has survived by keeping to its original brief and not deviating from the principles of its founder.

ABOVE **Pre-war tailoring in the best tradition by Maggy Rouff, 1940. Perennial Oxford grey flannel redingote – classic and perfect.**

# ROCHA, John

BORN: HONG KONG, 1953

A designer of Chinese and Portuguese parentage, John Rocha worked as a psychiatric nurse before moving to London in 1970 to study fashion at Croydon College of Design and Technology. He used Irish linen in his graduation collection and this prompted him to visit Dublin, where he opened a boutique for which he designed tailored linen suits. He has lived in Dublin for the past 20 years with his wife and business partner, Odette.

The Rocha look – which soon attracted international attention and led to him showing in Paris in 1994 – is plain, simple and covetable. It cleverly combines Oriental thinking with Irish craft. In addition to his fluid tailoring and work with linen, Rocha is also known for his use of rich, hand-painted fabrics, crocheted knitwear and sheer eveningwear. Rocha has worked in conjunction with Waterford Crystal, and produced complementary lines including John Rocha Jeans and John Rocha Home. He also collaborated on the concept and design of the Morrison hotel, which opened in the centre of Dublin in 1999.

# RODRIGUEZ, Narciso

BORN: NEW JERSEY, USA, 1961

Narciso Rodriguez was catapulted out of obscurity and into the forefront of the media when, as a complete unknown, he was commissioned to design Carolyn Bessette's wedding gown for her marriage to John F Kennedy jnr in 1996. The result was a triumphant combination of satin-backed crepe and supremely understated, elegant design. The famous shot of the stunning new Mrs John Kennedy, with her handsome husband kissing her hand, kick-started days of press speculation about the designer of the most significant wedding dress of the decade.

Bessette and Rodriguez met while working together at Calvin Klein – Bessette as a publicist, Rodriguez as a design assistant. Their friendship extended beyond working hours and culminated in the commission of a lifetime.

Son of a Cuban longshoreman and brought up in an unsalubrious area of New Jersey, Rodriguez studied fashion at Parson's School of Design in New York. It was while he was working as design consultant at Cerruti in 1997 that he was offered the position of design director at Loewe. He accepted the job, and continued to produce his own line in conjunction with Alberta Ferretti's Italian manufacturing base.

# ROUFF, Maggy

BORN: PARIS, FRANCE, 1896
DIED: PARIS, FRANCE, 1971

Maggy Rouff had a natural induction into the fashion world as both her parents were directors of the house of Drécoll and it was there that she learnt her trade. Rouff founded her own house in 1928, and gained a reputation for dazzling eveningwear, which she designed using fabrics normally associated with lingerie. She also designed lingerie, daywear and sportswear.

By 1950 the business was headed by Rouff's daughter, the Countess d'Arncourt. 'The house has a great feeling for the details and elaborately contrived evening dress, and has won great favour among Paris matrons,' commented *Vogue* in 1950. The house closed during the late 1960s.

# RYKIEL, Sonia

BORN: PARIS, FRANCE, 1930

One of the major figures in French fashion circles, Sonia Rykiel is best known for her chic knitwear, Left-Bank look, and stark white complexion, accessorized by her flame-red hair.

Despite having no previous commercial experience, Rykiel began her career as a freelance designer for Laura Boutique, which was owned by her husband Sam Rykiel. Even though she had an untrained eye, Rykiel's clothes had both aesthetic appeal and commercial clout – and she consequently opened her first Parisian boutique in 1968. Firmly established by the 1970s, and specializing in knitwear – especially fluid, often figure-hugging sweaters in soft wools and jersey – Rykiel then added menswear, childrenswear, cosmetics and a household line to her repertoire.

Rykiel has been honoured both in her own country – by the French Ministry of Culture – and abroad. In addition to a retrospective in Paris, she has had retrospectives in Tokyo and Luxembourg. Her clothes sell internationally.

Known as the 'Queen of Knitwear' in her homeland, as well as a cultural icon and multi-talented designer who can turn her hand to creating hotel interiors, corporate uniforms and children's books with equal success, Rykiel has launched three fragrances, the most recent of which is contained in a bottle designed in the shape of a sweater.

In 1998 Rykiel celebrated 30 years of working in the fashion industry and held a show which encapsulated her highly successful look. She also received a tribute in French *Vogue*.

ABOVE **A name that means French chic: Sonia Rykiel. Soft wool wrap-over jacket with frilled collar and gathered skirt, 1983.**

# SAINT LAURENT, Yves

**Born: Oran, Algeria, 1936**

Yves Saint Laurent – tortured genius, prolific inventor and owner of the century's most notable initials – spent his childhood in the searing heat of Oran, making paper theatres and costumes for his sister's dolls and dreaming of living in Paris.

Known as 'The Saint' in fashion circles, Saint Laurent put his foot on the first rung of the ladder when he won a competition sponsored by the International Wool Secretariat in 1954, and was introduced to Christian Dior by *Vogue*'s Michel de Brunhoff. He was then hired by Dior to work alongside him as a design assistant. Two years later, after Dior's premature death, 21-year-old Saint Laurent was thrust into the limelight. More than a mere hemline issue, his first collection was a life or death situation. The verdict was unanimous: 'Saint Laurent has saved France.' That said, his collection for Dior was a radical departure from the refined femininity and curvaceous tailoring of its founder. Saint Laurent spiced it up, producing Trapeze lines and, in 1960, the Beat Look, which shocked his more conservative customers but thrilled the Left Bank. Saint Laurent was conscripted into the army in 1960 but discharged after two months due to ill health. In 1962 he founded his own house and by 1969 he was a walking contradiction: infatuated by fashion, but pulled into artistic pursuits. *Vogue* was heralding the YSL signature as 'the most sought after look of today', but Saint Laurent felt pulled apart: 'I wish I could break my fingers when I think of what my love for sewing and dressing has become. But it was always there,' he said.

Saint Laurent's temperament has always been more suited to creativity than to business. His fortuitous partnership with Pierre Bergé has allowed him to design without the financial stress, and business has been crucial to Saint Laurent's success. In addition, Bergé's direction enabled Saint Laurent to become one of the first fashion designers to successfully reinvent his look – from couture to ready to wear. His second line, a ready-to-wear line, Rive Gauche, was a triumph. In 1970 Saint Laurent shocked the world by posing nude in an advertising campaign. On celebrating his thirtieth anniversary at the Opéra de la Bastille in Paris in 1992, Saint Laurent was joined by his friend, Catherine Deneuve, a long-standing customer. All his genius and inspiration was on display, including his homage to Léon Bakst's designs for the Ballet Russes, and to Piet Mondrian. There was also his masterly Le Smoking jacket, the feminized tuxedo, with just the right amount of angles and curves, and his beautiful vintage season jackets, immaculately embroidered with glittering vineyards by Lesage.

After over 30 years of creating immaculate clothes, Saint Laurent still designs the couture. In 1998 Alber Elbaz was appointed artistic director, followed by Tom Ford two years later on.

**OPPOSITE Yellow and smokily pale ostrich-feathered slip of flesh-coloured muslin, accessorized by barley sugar glass drop earrings, 1987.**

**ABOVE The unmistakable outline from Yves Saint Laurent's sketchbook of May 1986: polka-dot silk faille with silk crepe blouse and couture touches.**

# SANDER, Jil

**BORN: WESSELBUREN, GERMANY, 1943**

Jil Sander's clothes need no explanation, have no age limit and do not require accessories. Clean, precise and to the point, her minimalist style is based on design without decoration, perfect proportions and fluid lines. Her collections have made her one of Germany's most prominent fashion designers and most successful businesswomen – her company carries an approximate price tag of $200 million.

It is telling that Sander studied textile design and was a fashion editor for American and German women's magazines, before becoming a freelance designer. Her combined skills in the making and marketing of clothes have culminated in one of the most successful labels of modern times. A believer in growing a label at a slow, steady pace, Sander opened her first

boutique in Hamburg in 1968. By 1975 she had launched her own label, and pre-empted Japanese designers by showing her work in Paris, soon achieving international popularity. Sander always talks about intelligence in conjunction with the clothes she designs, and has said categorically that her label is for 'women with brains'.

# SANT'ANGELO, Giorgio di

**BORN: FLORENCE, ITALY, 1936**
**DIED: NEW YORK, NEW YORK, USA, 1989**

Giorgio di Sant'Angelo shot to fame in the 1960s, wavered during the 1970s and 1980s and made a resounding comeback in 1989. Sant'Angelo started out with fantastical ethnic dresses and ended up spearheading the Lycra revolution. 'I'm an artist who works in fashion, an engineer of colour and form,' he told *Vogue*. 'The minute a designer adds a zipper, it becomes junk.'

Sant'Angelo spent his childhood moving between Florence and Argentina. He studied architecture, dabbled in ceramics and also worked at Walt Disney for three weeks. Sant'Angelo moved to New York in the early 1960s, designing textiles before moving on to jewellery. Impressed by his talent, *Vogue*'s editor, Diana Vreeland, sent him into the Arizona desert with fabric, scissors, tape, and the model Verushka, and told him to invent clothes. The end result was featured over four double-page spreads.

Sant'Angelo won the Coty American Fashion Critics' Award in 1970. In and out of favour, his last collection was the perfect comeback. 'One cannot lose talent,' he told *Women's Wear Daily*. 'If one is good, he is good.'

# SASSOON, Bellville

**FOUNDED BY BELINDA BELLVILLE AND DAVID SASSOON IN 1958**

The cumulative talents of Belinda Bellville and David Sassoon cornered the market in great British eveningwear. 'I've never gone over the top,' said Sassoon to *Vogue* in 1998, when he was celebrating 40 years in business. 'The customer comes

LEFT **Young, fresh, and produced for 'women with brains' – Jil Sander's silk satin dress, left, and wool cashmere dress, right, 1999.**

OPPOSITE **Javier Vallhonrat's 1990 shoot inspired by Rothko colours: Giorgio di Sant'Angelo's cobalt jersey bodysuit, indigo cloak and boots by Blahnik.**

# SCAASI, Arnold

BORN: MONTREAL, QUEBEC, CANADA, 1931

Arnold Scaasi had an illustrious induction into the fashion world: he studied fashion in Montreal and Paris, worked with Jeanne Paquin and milliner Lilly Daché, and returned to New York in 1951 to work with the inimitable Charles James. Like James, Scaasi's clothes make both a statement and an impact. His work is a slice of Parisian couture in the middle of Manhattan. His designs often start with a sculptural idea, rather than a notion of a seamline or detail, and his elaborate dresses make an entrance rather than an exit.

Scaasi launched his elegant collection at an odd time – the early 1960s. He staged a retrospective of his work in New York's Lincoln Center in 1975, and has dressed an assortment of social butterflies including Ivana Trump, Joan Rivers, Elizabeth Taylor and, most famously, former first lady Barbara Bush for her inaugural ball. Scaasi's clientele are women who enjoy high-profile lunches and live for their charity work.

# SCHERRER, Jean-Louis

BORN: PARIS, FRANCE, 1936

Initially training as a classical ballet dancer, Jean-Louis Scherrer switched to study fashion at the Chambre Syndicale de la Couture Parisienne. Scherrer was an assistant at Christian Dior during the 1950s, later working with Yves Saint Laurent. He moved to Louis Féraud before founding his own label in 1962. During the 1970s Scherrer's career took off: his clients ranged from royalty – Queen Noor and Baroness Thyssen, to actresses including Sophia Loren and Raquel Welch. *Vogue* called him 'The Aladdin of the Couture'.

Scherrer started his career concentrating on couture, formulating boutique and ready-to-wear lines by 1971. His forte was blending the exotic with the everyday, but his heart has always belonged to haute couture: 'You can use marvellous fabrics, have wonderful, impossible embroidery – in fact, be superluxe,' he told *Vogue* in 1974, 'and superluxe is what the couture is all about.' In 1992 Scherrer was fired from the house he founded due to 'unsustainable losses'. He was replaced by Erik Mortensen, who said: 'I will do Mortensen chez Scherrer. But I do have a very strong image of Jean-Louis Scherrer.'

first. You don't remain in business for 40 years if you don't sell.' On Belinda Bellville's retirement in 1987, Sassoon was joined by designer Lorcan Mullany.

Bellville Sassoon has a loyal clientele which has continued from generation to generation. The company dressed Diana, Princess of Wales in her early years – including outfits such as her sailor-collared going-away ensemble, red and white stripes for Ascot in 1981 and an embroidered evening dress which she wore on an official visit to Canada and which ended up in Christie's sale of her clothes in 1997. Sassoon also once made a bridesmaid's dress for the wedding of Princess Anne; called to Buckingham Palace for the fittings, he recalled to *Vogue* in 1998 the Queen's only comment on viewing the dress: 'Is it washable?' the monarch wanted to know.

BELOW **Cecil Beaton's sketch of Elsa Schiaparelli, 1931, wearing an elegant stencilled evening dress, 'accessorised with a little cape of goose feathers'.**

RIGHT **Schiaparelli's 'Classical contours', 1935: two gowns with Grecian lines and draped hoods – 'one wonders why more women don't follow this lead'.**

# SCHIAPARELLI, Elsa

BORN: ROME, ITALY, 1890
DIED: PARIS, FRANCE, 1973

Elsa Schiaparelli and the surrealist movement were an unstoppable force in the 1930s – the seminal moment when fashion and art came together – with the mutual massaging of the wearable and the unorthodox. Schiaparelli made her *Vogue* debut with a trompe l'oeil sweater in 1927 (the same year she opened her Parisian boutique on rue de la Paix): 'Chic, modern sweaters are, of course, triumphs of fitting and this one from Schiaparelli is an artistic masterpiece.' She worked with Salvador Dalì, Christian Bérard and Jean Cocteau. Schiaparelli progressed from sweaters to tailoring, with touches that made the observer look twice: pockets like drawers, lobster and acrobat buttons, and in 1936, leather bands painted to look like rippled ribbon. In 1934 she used 'Cosmic' fabric, which comprised two layers of rayon tulle in contrasting colours. Together, they gave a watered, wavy effect. Schiaparelli's hats encapsulated her extraordinary approach – among them a shoe hat suggested by Salvador Dalì and a wicker basket filled with cellophane flowers: 'only for life's lighter moments – for lunch, afternoon, or dinner when your spirits are extremely high.'

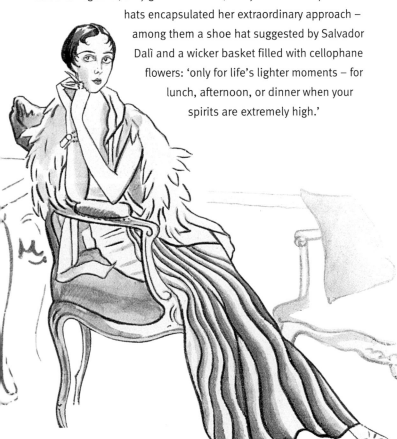

During the 1930s, Schiaparelli was the star whose ability to amuse put every other designer in the shade. Her perfume, Shocking, appeared in 1945. The bottle was based on the voluptuous curves of actress Mae West, for whom Schiaparelli had made a series of dresses including one in lilac broadcloth, and another in black tulle with pink taffeta roses and green leaves for her appearance in a play provisionally entitled *Sapphire Sal*. The following year she launched a perfume called The Roy Soleil in a glass bottle designed by Dalì. One of the first editions was sent to The Duchess of Windsor, Wallis Simpson.

In 1945 Schiaparelli was back in Paris after a four-year absence in America – 'the reception was of heartbreaking spontaneity, with tears of excitement, tears for all that had passed in the last four years and a childish faith that a miracle of inspiration, energy and production would now take place.' Her comeback was rapturously received.

Schiaparelli closed her house in 1954 and started to write her memoirs, fittingly entitled *Shocking Life*. In them she mused on alternative career paths that she could have taken, which included being a juggler, doctor, writer, cook, courtesan and a nun. She wrote *The Twelve Commandments for Women* which recommended shopping alone or with a man and included the cautionary advice: 'Remember – twenty per cent of women have inferiority complexes. Seventy per cent have illusions.'

# SCHÖN, Mila

**BORN: DALMATIA, YUGOSLAVIA, 1919**

Initially a customer of Cristobal Balenciaga, Mila Schön used the couturier's influence to start her own house in 1959 and quickly established it as an outfit that put quality before cost. Schön began to design menswear in addition to womenswear in 1972 and since then she has diversified into homeware, eyewear and jewellery. Referred to in the same breath as Fendi and Valentino, Schön's high level of quality is maintained by her refusal to compromise. In 1995, with a branch in Moscow, she was brought out of retirement to re-direct the house she founded.

# SHARAFF, Irene

**BORN: BOSTON, MASSACHUSETTS, USA, 1910**
**DIED: NEW YORK, NEW YORK, USA, 1993**

Awarded 16 nominations and five Oscars during her career, Irene Sharaff was best known for her ability to blend choreography with the demands of costume. She cut her teeth in repertory theatre, moving on to Irving Berlin musicals. From 1940 she worked on some of MGM's most popular musicals, including *Meet Me in St Louis* (1944). She was one of the designers on *Ziegfeld Follies* (1946) and *An American in Paris* (1951), where she created both sets and costumes for Gene Kelly's climatic ballet scene. Sharaff's other triumphs included *The King and I* (1956) and *West Side Story* – both the Broadway and film versions – during the early 1960s. She designed Pearl Bailey's costumes in *Porgy and Bess* (1959) and won an Oscar for her costume design for Elizabeth Taylor in *Cleopatra* (1963). Three years later she won her second Oscar, dressing Taylor in *Who's Afraid of Virginia Woolf?* (1966).

# SITBON, Martine

**BORN: CASABLANCA, MOROCCO, 1951**

Maker of colourful modern clothes with a historical slant, Martine Sitbon is one of France's best-known exports. She studied at the Studio Bercot in Paris and then travelled extensively, returning to Paris to produce her first collection in 1985. Two years later she took over from Karl Lagerfeld at Chloé and designed there for nine seasons.

The first Martine Sitbon shop opened in Paris in 1996. Today, she continues to design her own line – including eyewear – and keeps to the original design directive she devised in the mid-1980s.

# SMITH, Graham

**BORN: BEXLEY, ENGLAND, 1938**

One of Britain's foremost milliners, Graham Smith studied at Bromley College of Art, before moving to the Royal College of Art in London. Following his graduation, he went straight to Paris to take up the position of chief milliner at Lanvin.

Smith made the cover of *Vogue* in March 1965, with a pink silk twill hat decorated with huge spots. (A striped version was commissioned by Elizabeth Taylor, who was staying at the Dorchester at the time.) From 1981–98, Smith worked with Europe's largest hat company, Kangol. He collaborated with Jean Muir on her collections and with photographer Norman Parkinson on his Pirelli calendars. His royal productions have included a maple leaf hatpin for the Duchess of York, and a white sailor hat for Diana, Princess of Wales.

Smith celebrated 30 years of hat-making in the summer of 1989, when he confessed that he felt no affinity to Ascot. 'I've only ever been once,' he told *Vogue*. 'Not my cup of tea. Can't be doing with those penguin suits.'

# SMITH, Paul

**BORN: NOTTINGHAM, ENGLAND, 1946**

The shrewdest and most successful designer Britain has ever produced, Paul Smith founded his first shop – which was open on Friday's and Saturday's only – on Byard Lane in Nottingham in 1970, where he sold his own work as well as clothes by other designers. He presented the first Paul Smith collection in Paris in 1976, opened his first London shop in Covent Garden in 1979, and introduced womenswear in 1994. Smith, who enjoys worldwide success, currently has an annual turnover of $173 million, and over 200 branches in Japan. 'Persuasion or flattery is one skill,' he told the *Independent*, 'but not letting people down afterwards is another. You've got to deliver the goods.'

With no conventional training, Smith has become a multi-millionaire and Japanese icon. Through thinking logically, understanding his customer and never going over the top

OPPOSITE **Layering one jacket on top of another in Paul Smith's early foray into womenswear – slim lines and ankle boots elongate the silhouette, 1994.**

in his designs, his business offers a retailing benchmark to other traders. It also includes essential ingredients such as consistent high quality, clever marketing and a quirky sense of humour. In addition, Smith has never been guilty of trying to run before he could walk.

Smith's accolades include an honorary degree from Nottingham Polytechnic and a Royal Designers for Industry Award. In 1994 he was awarded a CBE, and the following year the Queen's Award for Export. In 1992 he declined a British Designer of the Year nomination.

Paul Smith's CV is a roll call of retail openings, achievements and exhibitions. In 1998 he opened the stunning Westbourne House in Notting Hill, London, an eclectic cross between a shop and a home, selling made-to-measure suits, antique clothes, amusing nick-nacks and Smith's own fashion lines, including his best-known item – his signature shirts in unconventional colours and patterns.

# SPROUSE, Stephen

BORN: OHIO, USA, 1953

Unusually for a designer with avant-garde leanings, Stephen Sprouse started his career at the refined end of the American market, working with two of its most famous names – Roy Halston and Bill Blass. Sprouse took the influence of London punk, which was prevalent in the late 1970s, and reinterpreted it, American style.

A high-profile figure in New York's social scene during the 1980s, Sprouse secured his name when he collaborated (like Vivienne Westwood) with artist Keith Haring, and was best-known for his stage clothes for stars of the rock world including Mick Jagger and Iggy Pop. He initially came to fame after dressing Debbie Harry during her Blondie period in the 1970s. Her peroxide hair was the perfect accessory for the day-glo colours –especially hot pink and yellow – favoured by Sprouse. Poised for a comeback in 1990, Harry candidly told *Vogue*: 'Before I met him I was a total mess. Don't ask what I wore. First I was a hippy, then it was cowboy boots and forties' dresses.' Sprouse provided the direction, the dresses and the colour, while Harry – with her unmistakable angular cheekbones – did the rest.

OPPOSITE **Stephen Sprouse's 'superhero' outfit, ready for take-off in silver leather, with matching boots and lots of functional details, 1984.**

# STARZEWSKI, Tomasz

BORN: LONDON, ENGLAND, 1961

The son of Polish refugees, Tomasz Starzewski is one of the designers who has breathed new life into British couture. He started his own business after he was expelled from London's Central Saint Martins College of Art and Design for staging an alternative fashion show. Starzewski began at the top, making Victoria Lockwood's fur-trimmed wedding dress for her marriage to Charles Spencer, as well as suits for Diana, Princess of Wales, a cocktail dress for Camilla Parker Bowles and, most recently, a steel-grey engagement suit for the Countess of Wessex. His clients are ladies who lunch, European royalty, and the occasional singing diva: Shirley Bassey often sits in his front row. In addition to couture, he produces men's and women's ready to wear.

Starzewski's forte is colour and shape – the cocktail dress, the classic suit, the jewel-buttoned jacket in which the wearer glides seamlessly from lunch to dinner, from fundraiser to racecourse. He puts himself in the same league as the Parisian and New York superpowers: 'I am the client's designer like Saint Laurent, Givenchy and Oscar,' he insisted in *Tatler* in 1991. 'We all give the customer what she wants.' In spring 1999 Starzewski switched his allegiance from London Fashion Week, to show in New York.

# STEELE, Lawrence

BORN: HAMPTON, VIRGINIA, USA, 1963

Born into a military family who travelled extensively throughout his childhood, Lawrence Steele graduated with a fine arts degree from the Chicago Art Institute in 1985. He became assistant designer at Moschino from 1985–90, leaving to collaborate with Miuccia Prada on the women's collection. His first collection was presented in 1994 and shown in Italy, with a knitwear line two years later. In 1999 he launched Lawrence Steele Design – a new range of technical active wear for both men and women. It blends what he does best: a mix of sportswear with an elegant edge.

# STIEBEL, Victor

BORN: DURBAN, SOUTH AFRICA, 1907
DIED: LONDON, ENGLAND, 1976

Victor Stiebel started his fashion career as a student at Cambridge University, where he followed in Norman Hartnell's footsteps, designing costumes for the Footlights revue. He trained at Reville and Rossiter before opening his own salon in 1932; two years later he was being compared to Digby Morton, Norman Hartnell and Charles Creed. Interrupted by the Second World War, during which he served in the British army, he took up employment at Jacqumar before reopening his own business in the more favourable economic climate of the 1950s.

Famous for his romantic dresses and thespian clientele, Stiebel had a superb eye for proportion – often experimenting with the positioning of stripes, plaid and accordian pleats to incredible effect. He could also effortlessly switch his talents from couture to mass-market. During his career he designed uniforms for the Wrens, as well as making elongated evening gowns for members of London's theatrical fraternity, in particular Vivien Leigh.

# STOREY, Helen

**BORN: LONDON, ENGLAND, 1959**

The eldest daughter of David Storey, author of the best-selling novel *This Sporting Life* (1982), Helen Storey made her mark on British fashion during the late 1980s. 'She became tremendously streetwise, largely through mixing with some rather alarming people,' her father remarked to *The Sunday Times*.

Storey graduated from Kingston Polytechnic in 1981, and worked at Valentino in Rome before producing her first collection under the Amalgamated Talent organization in 1984. In 1987 she joined forces with fellow designer Karen Boyd and opened Boyd and Storey in Soho.

By March 1990 the pair had gone their separate ways, and Storey's solo collections veered more towards the esoteric. Her spring/summer 1991 collection was entitled 'Rage', and she admitted to the *Daily Telegraph*: 'It's morally difficult for me just to design a frock.' In 1995 Storey showed her collection in a London Underground station, and her business went into receivership. She wrote her autobiography, *Fighting Fashion*, in 1996, in which she reflected, 'The tunnel was on the way to somewhere else, but I have yet to arrive.'

# SUI, Anna

**BORN: DEARBORN HEIGHTS, MICHIGAN, USA, 1955**

Anna Sui studied at Parson's School of Design in New York, but left after two years to work as a design assistant in a sportswear firm. Heavily influenced by the American take on punk, Sui

assisted Steven Meisel in the styling of his photographs. In 1980 she produced a capsule collection of six pieces, which were picked up by Macy's. Following her discovery by the New York department store, Sui started running her own business from her apartment.

By 1987 she decided to get more serious about design and found a manufacturing base. She made her first solo fashion statement in 1991, described by *The New York Times* as, 'a pastiche of hip and haute styles'. The winner of the coveted CFDA Perry Ellis Award for New Fashion Talent in 1993, Sui's celebrity clients include Courtney Love, Stevie Nicks and Lisa Marie Presley. Her favourite band is the Smashing Pumpkins.

# TARLAZZI, Angelo

**BORN: ASCOLI PICENO, ITALY, 1942**

A former student of political science, Angelo Tarlazzi switched to fashion in 1961 when he joined the house of Carosa to design eveningwear. In 1966 he relocated to Paris, assisting Michel Goma at Patou. He left to pursue a freelance career in America before rejoining Patou as artistic director, and finally opening his own house in 1978. The Tarlazzi look is unconventional and free-flowing. In common with the American minimalists, his clothes combine practicality with fluidity.

# TATSUNO, Koji

**BORN: TOKYO, JAPAN, 1964**

Maker of singularly unique pieces, which he described in 1990 as 'eclecticism in cloth … a spontaneous, non-academic approach which displaces the expected', Koji Tatsuno mixes cultures, antique textiles and touches of the unexpected in order to produce collections that combine modernity and history, tailoring and sculpture.

Tatsuno dropped out of school at the age of 14; by the time he was 18 he was living in London (although he spoke no English), and making clothes from antique fabrics. His recycled pieces caught the imagination of the buyers at Browns.

In the mid-1980s he designed under the Culture Shock label, followed by John Galliano, Paul Smith and John Richmond. His first salon in Mayfair, initially backed by Yohji Yamamoto, specialized in blending the sartorial antique with the bespoke coat – and employed a fledgling pattern cutter called Alexander McQueen, who had trained on Savile Row.

# THOMASS, Chantal

**BORN: PARIS, FRANCE, 1947**

Very French, extremely colourful and internationally renowned for its ability to suit every fashion capital, the Chantal Thomass label is one of France's greatest exports. Thomass started her career by making simplistic dresses out of silk scarves. In 1967 she formed her own company with her husband; nine years later it was re-christened Chantal Thomass. Now known as much for her lingerie as her outerwear, Thomass specializes in beautiful lace, feminine shapes and typical Parisian chic.

# TREACY, Philip

**BORN: COUNTY GALWAY, IRELAND, 1967**

Philip Treacy is the master of fantastical hats that suit statuesque supermodels and attract flashbulbs like a moth to a flame. His millinery extravaganzas have included a swirl of felt with a feathered monocle, and a sailing ship constructed from feathers.

Treacy trained at the Royal College of Art in London, where his final collection was a first-class celebration of the most difficult craft in fashion, a skill which he says is 'the nearest thing to mathematics'. He has lost count of the collections he has collaborated on – starting in 1991 with Victor Edelstein and Marc Bohan for Norman Hartnell. Now his roll call of co-designers is a who's who, ranging from Karl Lagerfeld to John Galliano. His celebrity clients run the gamut from Oscar winners to It Girls. Most commonly spotted on the runway and at racecourse meetings or society weddings, Treacy's hats are celebrations of incredible shapes.

Treacy has reinvigorated an industry which was sadly lacking in publicity. His technical team is unrivalled. 'Millinery is full of secrets,' he told *Vogue* in 1991. 'It's about tricks, and someone has to be generous enough to show you them.'

# TRIGÈRE, Pauline

**BORN: PARIS, FRANCE, 1912**

Pauline Trigère is credited with putting French elegance into Manhattan, and for rarely being seen without her trademark shades. The daughter of tailors, Trigère married a clothing manufacturer and learnt about fashion in the best way possible – through first-hand experience. For decades she was a symbol of French chic, chanelling her creative energy more into couture than ready to wear.

ABOVE **Philip Treacy's fantastical galleon: Seventeenth-century French sailing ship hat in satin with pheasant feather bones.**

In 1994, still elegant at 82 years of age, she started to concentrate on accessories. 'I'm only designing things you don't have to alter. I just got tired of sizing things,' she said. Winner of two Coty Awards, and an avid collector of turtles – the Chinese symbol of longevity – Trigère celebrated her fiftieth anniversary in business in 1992. When asked her age, she told *The New York Times*, 'I'm past 75. I still walk and I don't dye my hair blonde, and I don't touch it up.'

# TYLER, Richard

**BORN: SUNSHINE, AUSTRALIA, 1946**

Son of a seamstress, Richard Tyler trained as a tailor before opening his own shop, Zippity-doo-dah, in Melbourne with his mother in the late 1960s. By 1970 he was known on the rock circuit – his clothes were bought by Cher and Rod Stewart for his Blondes Have More Fun tour in 1978. Tyler eventually opened his own shop in 1988, and was fêted by the resident rock fraternity, selling his

clothes to Diana Ross and Ozzy Osbourne. He later admitted to *Vogue*: 'I got the leopard skin out of my system with Rod Stewart.'

In 1993 – by now in his mid-40s – Tyler won the CFDA Perry Ellis Award for New Fashion Talent; in the same year he became head designer for the Anne Klein label, describing his new appointment as 'a dream come true'. The collaboration lasted a year. Tyler now designs for Italian label, Byblos, in addition to producing his own range – Richard Tyler Couture and Richard Tyler Collection.

# UNGARO, Emanuel

**BORN: AIX-EN-PROVENCE, FRANCE, 1933**

Sizzling colour, feminine shapes and wild flowers are the signatures of Emanuel Ungaro, Italy's master colourist, and a resident in Paris.

As a child, Ungaro's first toy was not the expected train set but a Singer sewing machine. His father taught him how to use it and by the age of 13 he was working in the family business. He worked with Cristobal Balenciaga, whom he called 'the father of modern couture', and then briefly for André Courrèges. He established his own label in 1965, producing a look which was a combination of the two designers – Balenciaga's discipline with Courrèges's appreciation of youth. The look which Ungaro developed concentrated on his love of colour, floral prints and sinuous shapes; he often includes draping and appliqué. His Ungaro Parallèle line, which made its debut in 1968, centres on clear blocks of colour and classic shapes. 'You get surprises as you work with the fabrics, with ideas,' he told *Vogue* in 1974. 'And, of course, the surprises are essential – although they can often be bad surprises.'

Ungaro celebrated his twenty-fifth anniversary in 1990 at the Pavillon in Paris. At the same time he launched a book that despaired of the way in which the industry was going. 'Couturiers have been turned too much into stars! Who knows if that is not going to recoil on them?' That said, Ungaro was more than happy to feature his celebrity clients, including Texas socialite Lynn Wyatt and actress Anouk Aimée, in a series of Ungaro advertisements. He also made the floral wedding dress for Raine Spencer (stepmother of Diana, Princess of Wales) for her marriage to the Count de Chambrun. 'I adore the British,' he once said, 'they are the strangest people in the world and certainly the most exotic. And they do strange things too.'

LEFT **A native Australian resident in America, Richard Tyler's suiting is worn on and off stage by a variety of rock icons. Here, on the catwalk, 1995.**

OPPOSITE **'Paris couture as you would expect it to be', 1995: Ungaro's extravagant silk taffeta ballgown with sweetheart neckline and crinoline skirt.**

# VALENTINO

### BORN: VOGHERA, ITALY, 1932

Like his movie-star namesake, Valentino is a talent of gargantuan proportions, an Italian icon for whom an entourage and red-carpet treatment come as standard. He is not exclusively synonymous with glamour – his name gives subliminal messages of his signature colour, red, described by art historian Federico Zeri as, 'Not cardinal red, not tango red, but Valentino red.'

Born Valentino Garavani, he studied French and fashion design at Milan's Accademia dell'Arte before perfecting his technique at the Chambre Syndicale de la Couture Parisienne. In 1950 Valentino assisted Jean Dessès, the Greek couturier who specialized in draping, for five years. He moved on to Guy Laroche and assisted Princess Irene Galitzine before establishing his own business in 1960 on Rome's Via Condotti. His first collection was shown two years later.

Valentino's 'White' collection – unveiled in 1968 – generated sufficient press attention to make his name. He dressed Jacqueline Kennedy (publicly wooing her from Oleg Cassini) for her marriage to Aristotle Onassis. In 1991, Elizabeth Taylor asked Valentino to design a dress for her eighth trip up the aisle. The creation had a plunging lace neckline and woven ribboned waist.

For Valentino, read lavish lifestyle, glittering friends and decades of mingling in the most illustrious company. He has homes in London's Knightsbridge, New York and Capri, as well as a villa on the outskirts of Rome and a chalet in Gstaad. The cherry on the cake is a 43-metre (140-foot) yacht in which to survey the world's oceans. Valentino's office is a six-storey, seventeenth-century Roman palazzo, and he always works with his favourite pugs by his side. Immaculately groomed and permanently tanned, he buys his ties from Turnbull & Asser, and his shoes from John Lobb. At the weekend he wears Ralph Lauren.

Valentino's creations – clothes are too nondescript a term – are for women with cleavages, curves and bottomless bank accounts. His forte is dressing the elegant partners of exceedingly rich men. He once said, 'I don't think any man in the world wants to go out with a woman dressed like a boy.'

In 1987 he presented a fashion show in his home town of Voghera. He celebrated 30 years in business in 1991 with a three-day spectacular – encompassing 1,600 guests at an approximate cost of $5 million. The extravaganza culminated in dinner at the Villa Medici, attended by a host of international high-profile guests including Nan Kempner, Nancy Kissinger, Gina Lollobrigida and guest of honour Elizabeth Taylor. Fellow designers Gianfranco Ferre, Emanuel Ungaro and Hubert de Givenchy also lent their support. Valentino, who has exhibited in California, Rome and New York, has dressed the who's who of showbusiness, diplomatic and social circles.

RIGHT **Valentino's design for ladies who lunch, socialize, and always want to look as feminine as possible: tailored jacket, stole and soft pleats, 1980.**

OPPOSITE **'The perfection of prettiness': Evangelista in Valentino's couture oyster chiffon evening dress with crossover bodice and sable shoulders, 1991.**

# VANDERBILT, Gloria

**BORN: NEW YORK, NEW YORK, USA, 1924**

During the 1970s, at the height of the flamboyant disco era, Gloria Vanderbilt's name, face and figure were associated with skin-tight jeans complete with gold-stitched logo. Her publicity campaign was so successful that, together with Calvin Klein, she momentarily put Levi's in the shade and set the trend for designer jeans.

Vanderbilt left school at the age of 17 and went on to marry a string of famous men. First was Hollywood agent Pasquale DiCicco, followed by conductor Leopold Stokowski, who was 40 years her senior, film director Sidney Lumet, and finally, writer Wyatt Emory Cooper, who died in 1978.

Heiress to one of America's largest fortunes, Vanderbilt did not need to work, but claimed, 'The only money that means anything to me is the money I make myself.' Her business was founded on a remarkable licensing strategy that turned its creator into a household name. It started with jeans, when Murjani International requested permission to license her name to their design – which were the bestselling jeans in America by the early 1980s – and later spread into home furnishings, fragrances, greetings cards, luggage and footwear. Vanderbilt crossed the line from fashion designer to stylish dietitian when she licensed her name to a low-calorie dessert. At the height of her success she was frequently mobbed when she made appearances to promote her derrière-hugging jeans.

# VAN NOTEN, Dries

**BORN: ANTWERP, BELGIUM, 1958**

Low key and low profile, Dries Van Noten is part of the Belgian contingent who formed the world's sixth fashion capital. Van Noten studied fashion at Antwerp's Royal Academy of Arts, and started his own company in 1985. It was not until the 1990s, however, that his label became sought after and his name synonymous with eclectic and desirable clothes.

Van Noten's designs are precious and antique in feel, considered and unique in thought. He has an extraordinary colour sense, a wonderful feel for fabric and the most mouthwatering way of mixing textures together. He constructs rather than deconstructs, layering one texture on top of another. Van Noten's collections have been described as bohemian and incurably romantic – and always contain a crossing of cultures.

Customers view his clothes as wearable works of art. His influences are as diverse as, 'a car in the right colour, an African woman in Antwerp with a turban and classical raincoat', according to a profile of him in the *South China Morning Post* in 1997. 'Really, for me, an image in a book can be more inspiring than three weeks' travelling,' he said. 'It's nice to have a glimpse and then fantasise.'

**LEFT Dries Van Noten, who is normally noted for his way with ethnic embroidery and antique effects, dilutes the look for the catwalk, February, 1997.**

**OPPOSITE Leading the fashion for mixing and matching, Van Noten layers textures and colours for a cross-cultural style that looks glamorously eclectic, 1996.**

# VERSACE, Gianni

BORN: REGGIO CALABRIA, ITALY, 1946
DIED: MIAMI, FLORIDA, USA, 1997

Like a riveting blockbuster, Gianni Versace brought sex, glamour and a star-studded line-up to fashion during the 1990s. His dresses – a mixture of curve, glitter and slink – were worn by supermodels, the world's celebrities and, after her divorce, Diana, Princess of Wales.

Versace was not an instant hit. He moved to Milan in 1972, working as a freelance designer for companies including Callaghan and Genny. His first solo collection was for Complice in 1975. On 28 March 1978, the Gianni Versace label was launched at the Palazzo della Permanente in Milan. Versace's brother, Santo, handled the business side. In 1979 Versace produced his first advertising campaign in conjunction with photographer Richard Avedon. This was an inspired move that was to prove a long-running collaboration.

Versace captured a corner of the market not known for its solidarity to one particular designer. A decade after its formulation, the Gianni Versace label was being worn by the world's most powerful rock'n'rollers – Bruce Springsteen, Sting, Prince, Eric Clapton and George Michael. He held court at his palatial residence, the Villa Fontanelle on Lake Como, dubbed 'Versace's Rock'n'Roll Palace' by *Vanity Fair*. Elton John became a close friend: 'He's a sweetheart,' Versace told *Vogue* at the time. 'For his last show he said, "I want a new image – but I'm too old to wear a Mickey Mouse jacket. So we did something simple but just left the little hat."' In a spoof on his previous advertising campaigns, Avedon photographed Elton John in Versace dresses for *The Sunday Times* – with the headline, 'Ciao Chubby'.

In 1990 Versace held his first haute couture show in Paris at the Ritz hotel. His turnover was 600 billion lire. He had 320 outlets. The Versace boutique on Los Angeles's Rodeo Drive made $500,000 in a single month. Versace, supported by his brother Santo, sister and muse Donatella, and her husband Paul Beck, had the world at his feet. Interviewed by *Women's Wear Daily* in 1990, he said: 'In Italy I cannot compete with anybody. There are only three designers who give me the energy to fight – Yves Saint Laurent, Christian Lacroix and Karl Lagerfeld.'

When Versace was tragically killed in Miami on 15 July 1997, his sister Donatella carried on, somehow managing to complete the collection they had been working on. 'I knew Gianni would have wanted me to continue,' she told *Vogue* in 1998.

'Yes, I could have walked away, never done another day's work, but as a housewife I'd be a disaster.' A benefit was held at the Metropolitan Museum of Art Costume Institute in New York to celebrate the life and work of Gianni Versace; it raised a staggering $2.3 million. 'To see so many of Gianni's friends in one of his favourite places on earth made me so happy,' said Donatella to American *Vogue*. 'The atmosphere in the room was festive and spiritual all night.'

ABOVE **Evening wraps 'that's one of the big bombshells of the season' by Madeleine Vionnet. Duventine cape over panne velvet dress, tied with cords.**

OPPOSITE **Flawlessly-cut Vionnet – 'no evening gown has greater elegance' – in pure white crepe Romain with asymmetric hemline and silk tassel, 1926.**

# VIONNET, Madeleine

BORN: CHILLEURS-AUX-BOIS, FRANCE, 1876
DIED: PARIS, FRANCE, 1975

The supreme sculptress, who turned fabric into the purest form of fine art, Madeleine Vionnet knew exactly why there was a gulf between drawing and the final product. Lines drawn on paper can never simulate the feeling of fabric on skin. Simplicity was the watchword. Naturally, her perfumes were called A, B, C and D.

Vionnet became a dressmaker's apprentice at the age of 11. She married at 18, divorced, moved to London and worked briefly with Kate Reill before returning to Paris to work with Madame Gerber at Callot Sœurs, then with Jacques Doucet in 1907. Vionnet was about to open her own house when the First World War broke out, so she delayed it until the winter of 1918. By the early 1920s Vionnet had relocated from rue de Rivoli to a private house at 50 avenue Montaigne. In 1923 she married a younger man, but they divorced 20 years later.

Although Vionnet did not invent bias-cutting, she was the undisputed doyenne of it. Her technique was unequalled – liquid in motion and the pinnacle of minimalist perfection. Using her favourite fabric – silk crepe Romain – Vionnet took the timeless shapes – circle, rectangle and triangle – and transformed them into fluid sculptures. These were counterpointed by her complicated structures, which flowed over the body, held together by a single seam. Madame Raymonde, a former hand in the workroom, who later worked at Hardy Amies, said: 'She was simplicity itself. There was no decoration. None whatsoever. One toile had one seam, another there was a balance mark here, there and everywhere and when you draw the balance mark together it forms an enormous bow. Now, that's what I call genius. It is sculpture.' Vionnet's talent extended beyond the creative stage: she ran an impeccably managed house, with ten models, a nurse and separate kitchens for the *vendeuse* and workgirls.

In 1939 Vionnet showed her last collection, but lived to be almost 100 years old. She is adored by contemporary designers including Azzedine Alaïa, Issey Miyake and Vivienne Westwood. With Cristobal Balenciaga, it was a case of mutual admiration. Vionnet was 'a genius', he said. 'No one has ever carried the art of dressmaking further.'

# VITTADINI, Adrienne

BORN: BUDAPEST, HUNGARY, 1944

Dubbed 'Knitwear Queen' in America, Hungarian Adrienne Vittadini studied at the Moore College of Art in Philadelphia, Pennsylvania, and won a scholarship to apprentice with Louis Féraud in Paris in

Vivier became hooked, and opened his own house in 1937. Although he was a creative force in his own right, he designed for many other shoemakers including François Pinet in France, Herman B Delman in the USA and Sir Edward Rayne in England. The association with Delman proved lucrative – by the late 1930s Vivier was living in New York. In 1947 he returned to Paris, collaborating with Christian Dior when he opened a complementary shoe range.

A retrospective at the Musée des Arts de la Mode in Paris in 1987 revealed Vivier as not just an incredibly consistent creator, but also as an innovator, explorer and experimentalist, working with plastic, and turning extreme curves and angles into feasible shoe designs.

## VON ETZDORF, Georgina

BORN: LIMA, PERU, 1955

One of the instigators in moving evening fabrics from night to day during the late 1980s, Georgina Von Etzdorf is a textile designer whose work is distinctive, colourful and always associated with quality. She graduated from Camberwell School of Art, London, and formed her own company in the country producing silk-screen printed velvets and silk twills. Her early designs centred on scarves and shawls, but she has since graduated into pyjamas and dressing gowns, using silk-screen printing techniques.

## VON FURSTENBERG, Diane

BORN: BRUSSELS, BELGIUM, 1946

Diane Von Furstenberg is the woman who launched the wrap dress. She also had the longest legs in the business, prompting Tom Ford of Gucci to tell *Vogue* in 1988: 'Diane Von Furstenberg is the sexiest woman I have ever met.'

Born plain Diane Halfin, she studied at the University of Geneva, before marrying Prince Egon Von Furstenberg in 1969, and relocating to America. Her new-found aristocratic status eased Von Furstenberg into the American fashion industry. Although she had no formal training, she possessed an innate understanding of people, places, occasions and social situations. In short, she knew her market to the extent that her signature wraparound dress became a bestseller, selling in droves when Diana Vreeland featured its uncomplicated jersey form on the pages of American *Vogue*.

1965. Vittadini relocated to New York, specializing in the knitwear divisions of sportswear companies. She launched her own label in 1979, offering a collection that spanned sportswear, childrenswear, petites and swimwear. Approximately 60 per cent of her collection concentrated on knitwear, and her bestseller sold 26,000 pieces in one season. Vittadini sold her company in January 1996 but remained as chairwoman. She resigned, with her husband and business partner Gianluigi, in 1998. The label continues under new management.

## VIVIER, Roger

BORN: PARIS, FRANCE, 1913

Roger Vivier studied sculpture at the École des Beaux-Arts in Paris, and became a shoemaker by default when he was invited to try his hand at making shoes at a friend's factory.

In 1972 Von Furstenberg opened a showroom on Seventh Avenue, and made the cover of *Newsweek* at the age of 29. For the next 18 years she rode the wave of fluctuating tastes, re-entering the fashion fray in 1990, swiftly finding a new generation of customers who could relate to her work: 'I never played with dolls, I never dreamt of getting married or having children. I dreamt about love, passion, seduction and a bohemian life,' she told *Vogue* in 1998. 'To me, the most important thing is freedom. The only way you can be free is if you don't lie to yourself or others and you assume responsibility for yourself.'

# VUITTON, Louis

### FOUNDED BY LOUIS VUITTON IN 1854

One of the world's most unmistakable signatures, the Louis Vuitton logo is associated with big cheques, Lear jets and international lifestyles. For over a century, Vuitton luggage has been criss-crossing the globe, adding credibility to its owners. The Vuitton speciality is for luxury containers that cause a stir in VIP departure lounges. From the perfect stitchwork to the shade of its leather, Vuitton epitomizes the French flair for impeccable craftsmanship.

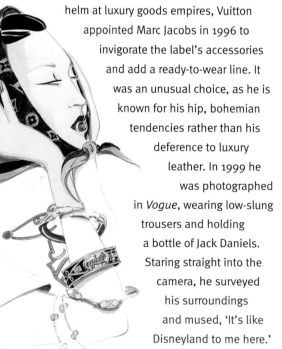

Echoing the trend for American designers to take the helm at luxury goods empires, Vuitton appointed Marc Jacobs in 1996 to invigorate the label's accessories and add a ready-to-wear line. It was an unusual choice, as he is known for his hip, bohemian tendencies rather than his deference to luxury leather. In 1999 he was photographed in *Vogue*, wearing low-slung trousers and holding a bottle of Jack Daniels. Staring straight into the camera, he surveyed his surroundings and mused, 'It's like Disneyland to me here.'

# WAKELEY, Amanda

### BORN: CHESTER, ENGLAND, 1962

Amanda Wakeley, who sums up her style in four words: 'modern, quiet, comfort, confidence', launched her own label in 1990. A former pupil at Cheltenham Ladies College, Wakeley worked as a house model in America for four years. Eveningwear is her forte, and she has won the British Fashion Award for Glamour three times and been nominated every year since 1993. Her first capsule collection contained her best-selling cashmere sweaters lined with silk satin. She now has a flagship store and two bridal collections, 'White Label' and 'Black Label', as well as her own collection and a range she designed with Principles.

# WALKER, Catherine

### BORN: AIX-EN-PROVENCE, FRANCE, 1945

Catherine Walker is the designer who made Diana, Princess of Wales look even more stunning than before. Taking her model proportions and photogenic looks, Walker transformed Diana from fashion plate to unforgettable presence. Always discreet, she understood that close inspection from all angles demanded a rigorous attention to detail.

Walker arrived in London from France with two baby girls, a British husband and a doctorate in philosophy. When her husband died shortly afterwards, she immersed herself in work, making children's and maternity clothes. In 1978 Walker established the Chelsea Design Company and although she had many famous clients – including Shakira Caine – it was the Princess who personified her eye for proportion. Dubbed 'Diana's Hidden Asset' by the tabloids, Walker dressed 'the dancing princess' in Australia, gave her a military suit to greet King Fahd, and a slinky navy number to complement her slicked-back hair at the CFDA Awards in New York. At the Christie's sale of Diana's dresses in 1997, out of 80 lots, 50 bore Walker's label. Ignoring the licensing deals and corporate contracts, she could make a million through her link with the Princess; but that's not her style. As she told *Vogue* in 1989: 'I'm not a commercial person at heart.'

# WATANABE, Junya

### BORN: JAPAN, 1961

A graduate from Tokyo's Bunka Fashion Institute, Junya Watanabe is best known as protégé of Rei Kawakubo, for whom he started to work in 1984. His design keeps to the Comme des Garçons aesthetic of pure lines, stark shapes and an appreciation of avant-garde cutting.

# WESTWOOD, Vivienne

### BORN: GLOSSOP, ENGLAND, 1941

Vivienne Westwood is England's most extraordinary ideas person. A revolutionary without equal and owner of a fertile imagination, she has unleashed punk, radical cutting, buffalo girls and underwear as outerwear, with bras worn over dresses, on an unsuspecting world. Only Westwood could defy logic by constructing a crown from scraps of Harris Tweed – the epitome of quirkiness, which became a Westwood bestseller. She despairs at the decline in elegance, the influx of American sportswear – faceless tracksuits and trainers – which she condemns as the 'brain-damaged look' of Britain's youth.

Born in a cottage in the Derbyshire countryside, Westwood was the eldest of three children. When she was 13, her parents bought Tintwistle post office. She went to Harrow Art School for one term before leaving to became a teacher and marry

Derek Westwood. At the age of 22 she had a son, Ben. She then met Malcolm McLaren, ex-manager of the New York Dolls and manipulator of the Sex Pistols, and in the early 1970s they also had a son, Joe. The meeting of minds produced the moment when fashion stopped, looked and listened. They opened a shop on London's King's Road at the height of the punk movement, selling fetishistic clothes in leather and rubber and tapping into the anarchic youth culture. Both the shop and McLaren's band brought the couple a great deal of media attention. When the split came, it was both professional and personal.

Westwood carried on alone, opening her shop, Nostalgia of Mud, and proving to her detractors that she was not a collaborator, but an inventor in her own right. The themes of her collections have continued to amaze and revolutionize – from her Pirate line with petti-drawers, ringlets and gold teeth in 1981 to her 'Buffalo Girls', 'Witches', 'Mini-Crini', 'Pagan', 'Anglomania' and 'Erotic Zones' collections. In 1992 she married her former design assistant, 27-year-old Austrian Andreas Kronthaler. Westwood's heroes are Christian Dior, Madeleine Vionnet and the writer Aldous Huxley. She uses and promotes British woven wools: 'I couldn't function as a designer without them,' she said in 1993, a year after receiving an OBE from the Queen, 'not only that, I wouldn't want to.'

Unquestionably one of the most influential figures in the fashion world, Westwood is a designer who reinvents, exploits and refuses to compromise. Her sexy, beautiful and sometimes outrageous clothes, although frequently criticized, are relentlessly copied – albeit in a more diluted form.

Known for her forthright opinions, anti-establishment views, disarming honesty and never wearing knickers in the presence of royalty, Westwood is funny, down-to-earth and devoid of any malice or fakery. She is a creative whirlwind, who rides a bike and doesn't give a damn about her detractors. Financial acumen is a common newspaper theme. But Westwood has always known her worth – and money never comes into it.

LEFT **Incorporating graffiti prints by Keith Haring, Westwood's tubular skirt; top, and Smurf hat sold in 1983 at her shop, Nostalgia of Mud.**

# WORKERS FOR FREEDOM

### FOUNDED BY RICHARD NOTT AND GRAHAM FRASER IN 1985

Originally founded by Richard Nott and Graham Fraser – who were named British Designers of the Year in 1989 and given their award by Diana, Princess of Wales – Workers for Freedom was a perfect balance of clean lines and crisp design, often with strategically placed embroidery. Their favourite combination was black and white.

Fraser studied accountancy and retailing, working for Harrods, the Wallis Group and Liberty, while Nott was a design assistant at Valentino in the early 1970s and a lecturer at the School of Fashion at Kingston University for a decade. The company re-located to France in 1993, intending to continue its more expensive clothing alongside the wholesale collection designed under contract with Littlewoods. However, the venture was short-lived and Workers for Freedom returned, showing in London a year later.

# WORTH,
## Charles Frederick

### BORN: LINCOLNSHIRE, ENGLAND, 1825
### DIED: PARIS, FRANCE, 1895

Regarded by many as the founder of Paris couture, English designer Charles Worth made fashion a personal issue when he used his wife, Marie, as his model after founding his house in the mid-nineteenth century. 'He conceived the idea of a dressmaking establishment where a woman should be dressed as befitted her type – an idea new to his day of impersonal methods,' noted *Vogue* in 1925.

Worth's mother was forced into domestic service when she was widowed. Her son, then 12 years old, was apprenticed to Swan & Edgar haberdashers. In 1843 he arrived in Paris with £5 in his pocket and secured a job with Gagelin & Opigez, selling accessories and fabrics. There, he met his wife Marie Vernet, a sales assistant, and started to dress her. Her new look began to attract compliments and eventually Worth's employers allowed him to have some floor space – in effect, his first designer concession.

Worth's talent was for instigating new trends, his fame for being the couturier of queens. He pushed the boundaries by employing a softly-softly approach to new sleeve variations, trimmings, colours and accessories (he pioneered the wearing of jet). Worth was also one of the first designers to show his creations on a house model rather than a static mannequin – a new device at the time. He shocked society by talking his wife into appearing at the prestigious Longchamp meeting wearing a dress without a shawl.

After the death of its founder, the house of Worth carried on under the direction of his sons and grandsons. Worth, the pioneer of Paris couture and precursor to Paul Poiret was, in *Vogue*'s opinion, 'very original, very much an artist, having opinions of his own and expressing them without fear or favour'.

LEFT **Worth's 'Chrysis' gown of georgette crepe, secured by an ornament of pearls, worn with a turquoise turban and hung with jet for dramatic effect, 1920.**

# YAMAMOTO, Kansai

**BORN: YOKOHAMA, JAPAN, 1944**

Theatrical, spectacular and designed for optimum visual effect, the creations of Kansai Yamamoto are rooted firmly in Kabuki theatre. Yamamoto studied English and engineering at Nippon University, and graduated from Bunka College of Fashion in Tokyo in 1967. He trained with Junko Koshino and Hisashi Hosono before leaving in 1971 to open his own company, where he had six employees and approximately $8,000 in the bank. Yamamoto showed in London and Tokyo and made a dramatic entrance with his initial appearance in Paris in 1975. He opened his first Parisian boutique two years later. Yamamoto also staged a show in New York in 1981 – choreographing his models movements and directing the action on stage from behind a mask – to rave reviews.

An artist at heart, Kansai Yamamoto has diversified into complementary lines which include clocks, stationery and ladies' shavers. These lucrative licensing deals have allowed him to satisfy his social conscience. For example, in 1998 he staged a cultural extravaganza called, 'Hullo India' at the Jawaharlal Nehru Stadium in New Delhi. Entry was free to the 40,000-strong audience – thanks to Yamamoto persuading Sony, Toshiba, Nippon and Canon to provide sponsorship – and included acrobatics, theatre and fireworks. Japan's best-known fashion designer staged the show (as he did in Russia and Vietnam) to touch the senses: 'I want as many people as possible to see them and say, "Wow!"'

**RIGHT Kansai Yamamoto's theatrical 'brocade for dressing-up nights': padded satin circus print, enormous platforms and every colour under the sun, 1971.**

BELOW **One of the most beautiful kimonos to come out of Japan: bias-cut navy blue silk printed with cherry blossom, 1994.**

# YAMAMOTO, Yohji

BORN: YOKOHAMA, JAPAN, 1943

'I have always liked asymmetry, both in design and in people,' said Yohji Yamamoto in 1990 – a statement that partly explains why the designer has always made clothes which are off kilter, question convention and kick-start the brain into overdrive.

Yamamoto's mother, a war widow, was forced to work as a dressmaker to provide for her only child. Yohji studied law at the University of Keio, but instead of pursuing a life of academia and legal wrangling, he switched to fashion, attending Bunka Fukuso Gakuin in Tokyo. He worked as a freelance designer before opening

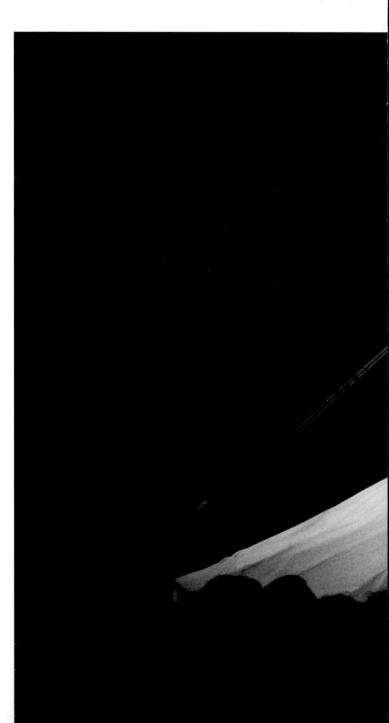

his business, Y Company, in 1971. His early collections consisted of woven cottons and linens – deep armhole dresses with Oriental cutting and kimono detailing. Yamamoto's turning point came in 1981 when he showed in Paris and caused a furore within the press corps. His clothes were called 'Oblique Chic' and 'Japantheon' by *Vogue* in 1983, and described as the 'art of the unexpected, mis-shapen, mis-matched lava textures, more calculated disarray with knotting, tearing and slashing: the provocation of paint-bruised make-up and high-strung hair'. Yamamoto wraps and drapes the body in unstructured, voluminous garments, but is less extreme than Issey Miyake and more understandable than Comme des Garçons. Rarely called a fashion designer, Yamamoto is more likely to be given the elevated title of poet, intellectual or artist.

He is a believer in mystique, an explorer of the relationship between fabric and body, and a leader of the avant-garde.

With Belgian deconstructivists on the warpath, Yamamoto was momentarily written off as too serious – passé, even. Yet he had come full circle. Pioneering, astounding and experimenting, his avant-garde take thrilled spectators but wasn't out of step. 'I like the idea that there's no beginning and no end, only today,' he told *The Sunday Times* in 1990. 'And that's enough.'

BELOW **Catwalk bride: Jodie Kidd in a gargantuan silk crinoline dress, her oversized hat held aloft by bamboo poles, 1998.**

# YUKI

**BORN: GNYUKI TORIMARU, MIZKI-KEN, JAPAN, 1937**

Master of drapery, Yuki is a Japanese minimalist working in England, who is best known for his refined, fluid, sculptural clothes. Originally trained as a textile engineer, Yuki was employed by an animation studio in Tokyo before moving to Britain in 1959 to learn English. He studied the history of architecture at the Art Institute of Chicago and then fashion at the London College of Fashion from where he graduated in 1966. Yuki worked with Louis Féraud, Michael Donellan and Norman Hartnell before spending three years in Paris with Pierre Cardin. He opened his own company in 1973 and presented his first collection to the Japanese in 1975.

Although he is best known for his dramatic, bias-cut eveningwear, frequently in silk jersey and designed to fall away from the body, Yuki has also produced swimwear and outerwear, often using soft jerseys, velvets and silk-jersey pleats. He has also designed costumes both for the theatre and television. Yuki enjoyed a renaissance when Diana, Princess of Wales diplomatically wore his dress for her state visit to

Japan for a dinner with Emperor Hirohito in 1986. The dress, constructed from perpendicular royal-blue pleating and embroidered at the neck and waist with blue bugle beads, raised over $25,000 at the Christie's sale in 1997.

In 1992 Yuki celebrated 20 years in fashion with a small retrospective at London's Victoria and Albert Museum.

# ZORAN

**BORN: BELGRADE, YUGOSLAVIA, 1947**

Creator of designs that are precise, clean, balanced and pure, Zoran is a minimalist who uses a predominantly neutral palette of black, white, ivory and pale grey with the occasional touch of red. His pared-down style consists of luxurious, silky tunics and fluid trousers in sumptuous fabrics such as cashmere and velvet – practical, comfortable clothing with longevity. He cuts simple shapes and avoids, wherever possible, the use of buttons and zips and any unnecessary decoration. Each of his pieces carries a sky-high price tag and the assurance of minimalist status. It is a label that is worn by Isabella Rosselini, Lauren Hutton and a coterie of Hollywood purists. *Vanity Fair* called Zoran's signature collection, 'Gap for the very rich'.

Zoran graduated from the University of Belgrade with a degree in architecture and moved to New York in 1971. His first collection, designed around squares and rectangles and launched in 1977 on the cusp of disco and the precipice of punk, caused a sensation – extreme purity in a sea of safety pins. His relaxed and sophisticated look has a timeless quality. Today, he's still hot: 'He's at the very top,' Philip B Miller, chairman of New York department store, Saks Fifth Avenue, told *The New York Times* in 1999.

Exclusive and covetable, Zoran has resolutely kept to his original concept of working with a few capsule pieces, constructed from dimensions rather than drawings. He doesn't do drapery, bias-cutting or anything complex. In 1993 he told *The Sunday Times*: 'I hate long red nails. I don't like women who wear sunglasses indoors or high heels. Feathers belong on birds, not human beings.' In 1999 his annual sales were estimated at $25 million wholesale. Pure and simple.

**LEFT Yuki's 'softly softly silk', 1976, modelled by Jerry Hall; in cream jersey, the hem doubles up as a hood, the front is tucked at just the right point.**

**OPPOSITE Zoran's back to the future: his 'pure panache', 1986 white silk lamé, is cut in one piece and totally devoid of seams, with a single knot at the back.**

# INDEX

# USEFUL INFORMATION

GALLERIES & MUSEUMS

United Kingdom

Birmingham City Museum & Art Gallery
Chamberlain Square
Birmingham B3 3DH
(44 121) 303 2834

The Bowes Museum
Barnard Castle
Durham DL12 8NP
(44 1833) 690606

Brighton Art Gallery & Museum
Church Street
Brighton
East Sussex BN1 1UE
(44 1273) 29990900

The Cecil Higgins Art Gallery
Castle Close
Bedford MK40 3RP
(44 1234) 211222
www.beds.gov.uk

Costume & Textile Study Centre
Carrow House
301 King Street
Norwich NR1 2TS
(44 1603) 223870

Gallery of English Costume
Platt Hall
Rusholme
Manchester M14 5LL
(44 161) 224 5217

Grosvenor Museum
27 Grosvenor Street
Chester
Cheshire CH1 2DD
www.chestercc.gov.uk

Museum of Costume
The Assembly Rooms
Bennett Street
Bath
Avon BA1 2QH
(44 1225) 477789
www.museumofcostume.co.uk

Museum of Costume & Textiles
51 Castle Gate
Nottingham NG1 6AF
(44 115) 915 3541

Museum of Welsh Life
St. Fagans
Cardiff CF5 6XB
(44 1222) 573500
www.nmgw.ac.uk

National Museums of Scotland
Chambers Street
Edinburgh EH1 1JF
(44 131 225 7534)

Paisley Museum & Art Gallery
High Street
Paisley
Renfrewshire PA1 2BA
(44 141) 889 3151

Rowley's House Museum
Barker Street
Shrewsbury SY1 1QH
(44 1743) 361196

State Apartments & Royal
Ceremonial Dress Collection
Kensington Palace
London W8 4PX
(44 171) 937 9561
www.hrp.org.uk

Ulster Museum
Botanic Gardens
Stranmillis Road
Belfast BT9 5AB
(44 1232) 383000
www.ulstermuseum.org.uk

Victoria & Albert Museum
Cromwell Road
London SW7 2RL
(44 171) 938 8500
www.vam.ac.uk

York Castle Museum
York YO1 9RY
(44 1904) 653611

United States

The Arizona Costume Institute
The Phoenix Art Museum
1625 North Central Avenue
Phoenix
AZ 85004
(1 602) 257 1222
www.phxart.org

The Brooklyn Museum of Art
Eastern Parkway
Brooklyn
New York
NY 11238
(1 718) 638 4486

Chicago Historical Society
1601 Clark Street at North Avenue
Chicago
IL 60614
(1 312) 642 4600

The Costume Institute
Metropolitan Museum of Art
1000 Fifth Avenue
New York
NY 10028-0198
(1 212) 570 3908
www.metmuseum.org

The Fashion Institute of Technology
West 27th Street at 7th Avenue
New York
NY 10001-5992
(1 212) 217 7000

Indianapolis Museum of Art
1200 West 38th Street
Indianapolis
IN 46208- 4196
(1 317) 923 1331
www.ima/art.org

Kent State University Museum
Rockwell Hall
Kent
OH 44242
(1 350) 672 3450

Los Angeles County Museum of Art
5905 Wilshire Boulevard
Los Angeles
CA 90036
(1 213) 857 6000

The Museum of Fine Arts
465 Huntingdon Avenue
Boston
MA 02115
(1 617) 267 9300
www.mfa.org

Museum of the City of New York
1220 Fifth Avenue
New York
NY 10029
(1 212) 534 1672
www.mcny.org

Philadelphia Museum of Art
26th Street & Benjamin Franklin Parkway
Philadelphia
PA 19130
(1 215) 763 8100
www.philamuseum.org

Wadsworth Atheneum
Hartford
CT 06103
(1 860) 247 1831

Italy

Accademia di Costume e di Moda
Via della Rondinella 2
00186 Rome
(39 6) 686 4132
acc.dicostume.flashnet.it

Civiche Raccolte d'Arte Applicata
Castello Sforzesco
20121 Milan
(39 2) 869 3071
albertogasparini@cm.inet.it

Galleria del Costume
Palazzo Pitti
50125 Florence
(39 55) 239 8725

Museo Palazzo Fortuny
Camp San Beneto
3780 San Marco
Venice
(39 41) 520 0995

France

Musée de la Chemiserie et de l'Elégance
Masculine
rue Charles Brillaud
36200 Argenton-sur-Creuse
(33 2) 54 24 34 69
m.legance.masculena@friisbii.fr

Musée de la Mode et du Textile
Palais du Louvre
107 rue de Rivoli
75001 Paris
(33 1) 44 55 57 50
www.ucad.com.

Musée des Beaux-Arts et de la Dentelle
25 rue Richelieu
62100 Calais
(33 3) 21 46 48 40

Musée du Chapeau
16 route de Saint Galmier
42140 Chazelles-sur-Lyon
(33 4) 77 94 23 29

Musée des Tissus
30-34 rue de la Charité
69002 Lyon
(33 4) 78 38 42 00

Musée Galliéra
Musée de la Mode de la Ville de Paris
10 avenue Pierre Premier de Serbie
75116 Paris
(33 1) 47 20 85 23

Musée Internationale de la Chaussure
2 rue Sainte-Marie
26100 Romans
(33 4) 75 05 81 30

Canada

Bata Shoe Museum
327 Bloor St. West
Toronto
Ontario M5S 1W7
(1 416) 979 7799
www.toronto.com.batashoemuseum

McCord Museum
690 Sherbrooke Street West
Montreal
Quebec H3A 1E9
(1 514) 398 7100
info@mccord.lan.mcgill.ca

Royal Ontario Museum
100 Queen's Park
Toronto
Ontario M5S 2C6
(1 416) 586 8000
www.rom.on.ca

WEBSITES

www.bestofbritish.com
Designs from some of Britain's top
fashion names including Lulu Guinness
and Camilla Ridley.

www.bloomingdales.com
Online service from New York's
distinguished department store, where
many top designers gained their first
big opportunity.

www.brownsfashion.com
Everything from Fendi baguettes to silk
kimono eye rests and cashmere
sweaters for the dog who has
absolutely everything.

www.chanel.co.uk
Information and products from the House
of Chanel.

www.csm.linst.ac.uk
Courses and information about Central St
Martin's College of Art & Design.

www.thecrosscatalogue.com
Bohemian chic from The Cross in
London's Notting Hill.

www.elspethgibson.com
Elspeth Gibson is known for her
attractively feminine designs. Includes
a gallery of latest designs and news.

www.gucci.com
Products and information from Gucci.

www.handbag.com
Fashion, health and beauty sites.

www.Harrods.co.uk
Everything you would expect from
London's most luxurious store.

www.lauraashley.com
Classic clothing,including the famous
Laura Ashley prints.

www.tiffany.com
Luxurious jewels and helpful advice on
caring for jewellery and buying diamonds.

www.vuitton.com
Information and products from Louis
Vuitton.

www.yslonline.com
Information and products from Yves
St Laurent.

FURTHER READING

ANSCOMBE Isabelle, *A Woman's Touch:
Women in Design from 1860 to
the Present Day*, New York, Viking
Press, 1984
ASH Juliet and WILSON Elizabeth, *Chic
Thrills: A Fashion Reader*, London,
Pandora Press, 1992
AVEDON Richard, *Evidence 1944–1994*,
New York, Random House/Eastman
Kodak, 1994
BAINES Barbara, *Fashion Revivals*,
London, B.T. Batsford Ltd., 1981
BALLARD Bettina, *In My Fashion*, New
York, David McKay, 1967
BANNER Lois, *American Beauty*, New
York, Alfred A. Knopf, 1983
BARWICK Sandra, *A Century of Style*,
London, Allen & Unwin, 1984
BATTERBURY Michael and Ariane,
*Fashion. The Mirror of History*, New York,
Greenwich House, 1977
BATTERSBY Martin, *Art Deco Fashion*,
London, Academy Editions, 1974
BEATON Cecil, *The Magic Image: The
Genius of Photography*, London, Pavilion
Books, 1989
BRAIN Robert, *The Decorated Body*, New
York, Harper & Row, 1979
CARTER Ernestine, *The Changing World
of Fashion*, London, Weidenfeld
& Nicolson, 1977
—*Magic Names of Fashion*, London,
Weidenfeld & Nicholson, and Englewood
Cliffs, New Jersey, Prentice-Hall, 1980
CHAPSAL Madeleine, *La Chair de la robe*,
Paris, Fayard, 1989
COLCHESTER Chloe, *The New Textiles:
Trends & Traditions*, London, Thames &
Hudson, 1994
CORE Philip, *The Original Eye: Arbiters
of Twentieth Century Taste*, London,
Melbourne and New York, Quartet
Books, 1984
DARIA Irene, *The Fashion Cycle*, New
York, Simon & Schuster, 1990
DEVLIN Polly, *Vogue Book of Fashion
Photography*, London, Thames & Hudson,
and New York, William Morrow and
Co., 1979
DIAMONDSTEIN Barbaralee, *Fashion:
The Inside Story*, New York, Rizzoli
International, 1985
DIOR Christian, *Dior by Dior*, London,
Weidenfeld & Nicholson, 1957
DORNER, Jane, *The Changing Shape
of Fashion*, London, Octopus Books
Ltd., 1974
EVANS Caroline and THORNTON Minna,
*Women and Fashion: A New Look*,
London and New York, Quartet
Books, 1989
EWING Elizabeth, *History of Twentieth
Century Fashion*, London, B.T. Batsford,
1974
GAN Stephen, *Visionaire's Fashion.
Designers at the Turn of the Millenium*,
London, Laurence King Publishing, 1997
GINSBURG Madeleine, *An Introduction to
Fashion Illustration*, London, Victoria and
Albert Museum Publications, 1980

GLYNN Prudence, *In Fashion: Dress in the Twentieth Century*, London, Allen & Unwin, 1978

HAEDRICH Marcel, *Coco Chanel: Her Life, Her Secrets*, London, Robert Hale, and Boston, Little, Brown & Co., 1972

HALL-DUNCAN Nancy, *The History of Fashion Photography*, New York, International Museum of Photography/Harry N. Abrams, 1978

HAYE Amy de la (ed.), *The Cutting Edge. 50 Years of British Fashion. 1947–1997*, London, Victoria and Albert Museum Publications, 1996

HEBDIGE Dick, *Subculture: The Meaning of Style*, London and New York, Methuen Inc., 1979

HOWELL Georgina, *In Vogue*, New York, Schocken Books, 1975

HULANICKI Barbara, *From A to Biba*, London, Hutchinson, 1983

KHORNAK Lucille, *Fashion 2001*, New York, Viking Press, 1982

KRELL Gene, *Vivienne Westwood*, London, Thames & Hudson, and New York, Universe Publishing, Fashion Memoir, 1997

LACROIX Christian, *Pieces of a Pattern: Lacroix by Lacroix*, London and New York, Thames & Hudson, 1992

LENCEK Lena and GIDEON Bosker, *Making Waves: Swimsuits and the Underdressing of America*, San Francisco, Chronicle Books, 1989

LOBENTHAL Joel, *Radical Rags: Fashions of the Sixties*, New York, Abbeville Press, 1990

LURIE Alison, *The Language of Clothes*, London, Hamlyn Publications, 1982

LYNAM Ruth (ed.), *Paris Fashion*, London, Michael Joseph, 1972

—*Couture: An Illustrated History of the Great Paris Designers and Their Creations*, New York, Doubleday & Co., 1972

MADSEN Axel, *Living for Design: The Yves Saint Laurent Story*, New York, Delacorte Press, 1979

DE MARLY Diana, *The History of Haute Couture, 1850–1950*, London, B.T. Batsford, 1980

MARTIN Richard (ed.), *Contemporary Fashion*, Detroit, St James Press, 1995

McCONATHY Dale and VREELAND Diana, *Hollywood Costume*, New York, Harry N. Abrams, 1976

McDERMOTT Catherine, *Street Style: British Design in the 80s*, New York, Rizzoli International, 1987

McDOWELL Colin, *McDowell's Directory of Twentieth Century Fashion*, London, Frederick Muller, 1984

MENDES, Valerie D., *Twentieth Century Fashion: An Introduction to Women's Fashionable Dress, 1900 to 1980*, London, Victoria and Albert Museum Publications (exhibition catalogue), 1981

—(ed.), Pierre Cardin: *Past, Present and Future*, London and Berlin, Dirk Nishen, 1990

MILBANK Caroline Rennolds, *Couture, The Great Fashion Designers*, London, Thames & Hudson, and New York, Stewart, Tabori & Chang, 1985

—*New York Fashion: The Evolution of American Style*, New York, Harry N. Abrams, 1989

MORENO Elizabeth, *The Fashion Makers: An Inside Look at America's Leading Designers*, New York, Random House, 1978

MULVAGH Jane, *Costume Jewelry in Vogue*, London and New York, Thames & Hudson, 1988

—*Vogue History of 20th-Century Fashion*, Harmondsworth, Middx, Penguin Books Ltd, 1988

NUZZI Christina, *Parisian Fashion*, New York, Rizzoli International, 1980

O'HARA CALLAN Georgina, *Dictionary of Fashion and Fashion Designers*, London and New York, Thames & Hudson, 1998

PACKER William, *Fashion Drawing in Vogue*, London, Thames & Hudson, 1983

PALMER WHITE Jack, *Poiret*, London, Studio Vista, and New York, Potter, 1973

—*Elsa Schiaparelli*, London, Aurum Press, and New York, Rizzoli International, 1986

POLHEMUS Ted, *Pop Styles*, London, Vermilion, 1984

—*Street Style: From Sidewalk to Catwalk*, London, Thames & Hudson, 1994

—*Style Surfing: What to Wear in the Third Millennium*, London, Thames & Hudson, 1996

QUANT Mary, *Quant by Quant*, London, Cassell & Co., 1966

—*Colour by Quant*, London, Octopus Books Ltd., 1984

RHODES Zandra and KNIGHT Anne, *The Art of Zandra Rhodes*, London, Jonathan Cape, and Boston, Houghton Mifflin Co., 1984

RILEY Robert, *The Fashion Makers*, New York, Crown, 1968

—*Givenchy: 30 Years*, New York, Fashion Institute of Technology, 1982

ROBINSON Julian, *Fashion in the Forties*, New York, Harcourt Brace Jovanovich, 1976

—*The Golden Age of Style. Art Deco Fashion Illustration*, London, Orbis Publishing Ltd., 1976

—*Fashion in the Thirties*, London, Oresko Books, 1978

ROTHSTEIN Natalie (ed.), *Four Hundred Years of Fashion*, London, Victoria and Albert Museum Publications, 1984

SCHIAPARELLI Elsa, *Shocking Life*, London, J.M. Dent, and New York, E.P. Dutton, 1954

SEEBOHM Caroline, *The Man Who Was Vogue. The Life and Times of Condé Nast*, New York, Viking Press, 1982

STEELE Valerie, *Paris Fashion: A Cultural History*, Oxford and New York, Oxford University Press, 1988

—*Women of Fashion. Twentieth Century Designers*, New York, Rizzoli International, 1991

TATE Sharon Lee, *Inside Fashion Design*, New York, Harper & Row, 1984

VREELAND Diana (ed.), *American Women of Style*, New York, Costume Institute, Metropolitan Museum of Art (exhibition catalogue), 1975

## PICTURE CREDITS

The publishers would like to thank the following sources for their kind permission to reproduce the pictures in this book:

t: top, b: bottom, l: left, r: right, tl: top left, tr: top right, bl: bottom left, br: bottom right, bc: bottom centre, bcl: bottom centre left, bcr: bottom centre right.

All images © *Vogue*, The Condé Nast Publications Ltd.

Michel Arnaud 23, 55
Clive Arrowsmith 51
David Bailey 21
Cecil Beaton 29t, 29b
Maurice Beck & Helen Macgregor 12t
Eric Boman 28
Brad Branson 3, 49
Henry Clarke 4, 17
Patrick Demarchelier 1, 24, 39
Terence Donovan Archive 35
Brian Duffy 18
Rodger Duncan 46
Arthur Elgort 48
Robert Erdmann 31
Carl Erickson 10, 44
Anna Harvey 53
Andrew Lamb 36, 40, 41
Barry Lategan 14, 54
Andrew Macpherson 42
Tom Munro 15, 26, 43
Jacques Olivar 7, 47
Douglas Pollard 45
Yves Saint Laurent 24
Bert Stern 6
Mario Testino 37
Ronald Traeger 19
Javier Vallhonrat 26
Vittoriano Rastelli/Corbis (jacket)
Albert Watson 32
Martin Welch 8
Porter Woodruff 50

## ACKNOWLEDGEMENTS

Very special thanks to Erika Frei for her encouragement
and advice on the fine art of tact and diplomacy.
To Joyce Douglas for being there.

Thank you to Vogue's superb library staff
– Darlene Maxwell, Chris Pipe, Nancy Kim, headed by
the brilliant Lisa Hodgkins – for their support, good humour
and company throughout this project.

Two people who were fundamental: endless thanks
to Francesca Harrison, picture editor, for being calm,
efficient and having a lovely eye. Emily Wheeler-Bennett,
Condé Nast's editorial business and rights director,
for being a complete professional and friend.

This book is dedicated to my mother, father and
brother Billy with love.